Hoodoo Honey and Sugar Spells

Sweet Love Magic In The Conjure Tradition

by Deacon Millett

Lucky Mojo Curio Company
Forestville, California

2013

Hoodoo Honey & Sugar Spells:
Sweet Love Magic In The Conjure Tradition
by Deacon Millett
FourAltars.org

Text:
Deacon Millett

Cover:
Tony Link

Production:
catherine yronwode, nagasiva yronwode
Charles Wylie, Fred Burke

Illustrations:

Some material in this book appeared at the
Lucky Mojo Curio Company Forum
Forum.LuckyMojo.com
Used With Permission

First Edition 2013
Second Edition 2015
Third Edition 2017

Published by
The Lucky Mojo Curio Company
6632 Covey Road
Forestville, California 95436
LuckyMojo.com

ISBN: 978-0-9719612-4-1

Printed in Canada.

CONTENTS

Dedication

To the Lovelorn, Lovelost, and Brokenhearted.
Better to light one candle than to curse the darkness.

Acknowledgements

I first wish to thank my partner Matthew, without whom I would find myself in no position to write about love magic — much less practice it for others. I am so happy to have you in my life.

Thanks also to the wonderful members of the Lucky Mojo Forum, whose endless curiosity, questions, and desire to help others are a spiritual force to be reckoned with. A special tip of the hat to the Forum Moderators, who bring their expertise to the table every day.

Many of the answers herein were provided by colleagues from the Association of Independent Readers and Rootworkers:

Catherine Yronwode
ConjureMan Ali
Deacon Millett
Devi Spring
Dr. Johannes
Lukianos
Miss Bri
Miss Michaele

I am lucky to be a part of this Missionary Independent Spiritual Church outreach, and thank all my AIRR colleagues for their continued love and support.

My gratitude to Nagasiva, Susie, Don, Robin, Heidi, Alicia, and all the Lucky Mojo Curio Co. staff, past, present, and future, for sweetening my life and the lives of so many.

Most of all, I must thank Catherine Yronwode, my lifelong teacher and friend, for respectfully preserving the African-American art of conjure for myself and generations to come.

Hoodoo, Conjure, Rootwork

Hoodoo, also called conjure or rootwork, is an African-American folk magic tradition born in the crucible of American slavery, where ancient African magic met and merged with Protestant Christianity, Native American herbal lore, and a dash of European customs.

In the hoodoo tradition, we see several overarching practices. The first is sympathetic magic: A hair from your head is a part of you, and what is done to the part will affect the whole. Next is the "Doctrine of Signatures," a correspondence between the look, name, or attributes of an herb or object that help define its magical use. Thus lodestones, which are attracted to each other, promote attraction between people. Last, there is the call to the Spirit world, to ancestors, deities, and the dead. Their aid can help our endeavours.

After the Civil War, hoodoo travelled northward, assimilating Asian, Jewish, and Spiritualist ideas, adding seals, grimoires, and lucky perfumes. By the 20th century, hoodoo goods were sold by mail order across the USA.

Hoodoo is a uniquely American creation, like jazz and comic books, in which a fusion of traditions comes together as something greater than the whole. And it continues to grow. When glass-encased candles came into use in the 1970s, rootworkers quickly added them to the repertoire. If it *works* and makes *sense*, then hoodoo workers will take a look.

What Hoodoo is Not

Hoodoo is not a religion. It is definitely not Voodoo, a West African religion with offshoots in Haiti, Puerto Rico, and Brazil.

Hoodoo does not have a hierarchy, and there are no initiatory rituals.

Hoodoo does not carry with it a belief in "karma" or a "three-fold law of return." It is not Wicca, or Neo-Paganism, or "New Age."

Hoodoo is not Black Magic, and most hoodoo spells and rituals are done in the name of Jesus or the Father, Son, and Holy Spirit.

If hoodoo has an official book, it is The Bible.

For more on the history of Hoodoo see:
LuckyMojo.com/hoodoohistory.html
Southern-Spirits.com
"Hoodoo Herb and Root Magic" by Catherine Yronwode

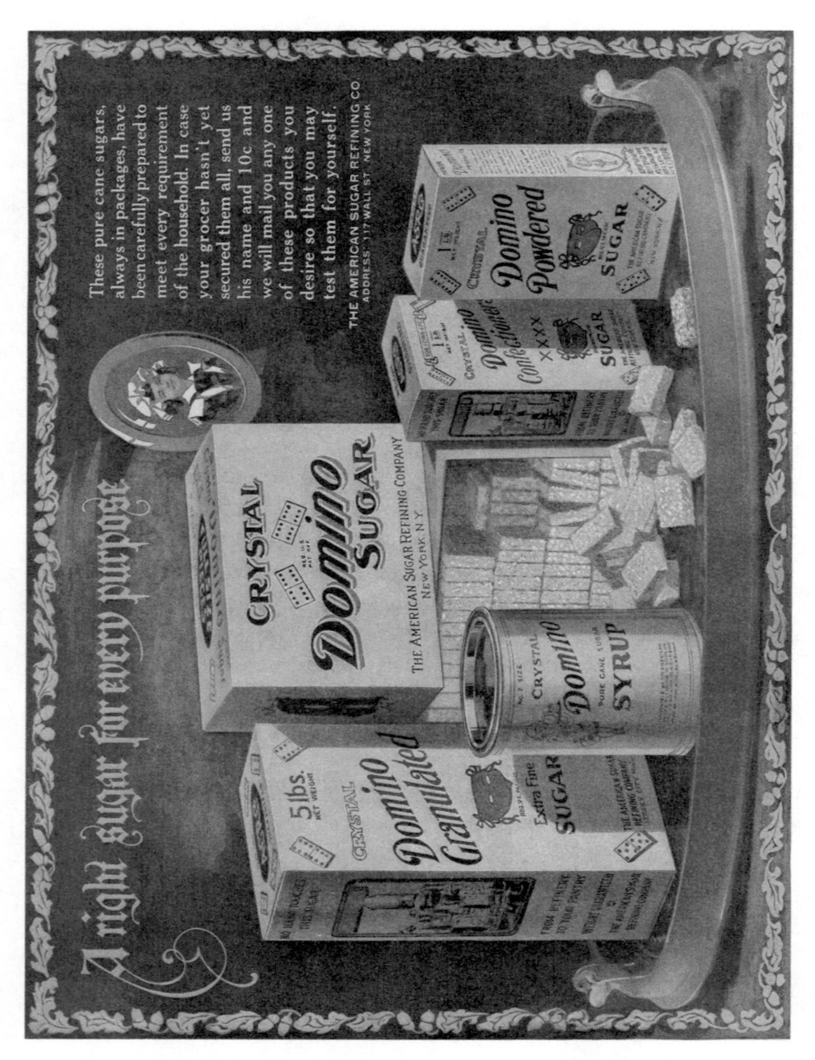

1914 advertisement from The Ladies' Home Journal.
Domino Sugar products from the American Sugar Refining Co.,
displaying the brand's trademarked domino-shaped "sugar cubes,"
as well as lucky dominos and domino masks on the packaging.

The Right Sweetener for Every Purpose

A myriad of sweeteners have been used in hoodoo, from plain ol' table sugar to the honey in vogue today. And, just as in cooking, each one has its time and place. Old-time conjure doctors chose the colour of the sugar based on the skin colour of the target, but this has thankfully fallen out of favour. We have many sweetening options today.

- **Granulated Sugar**: Refined white sucrose ready for a sugar bowl.
- **Brown Sugar**: Varies in colour and strength of flavour, depending on the amount of molasses added.
- **Confectioners Sugar**: A light powder, used for dusting or icings.
- **Superfine Sugar**: Easy to dissolve in drinks or for simple syrup.
- **Sugar Cubes**: Lump sugar and longer bricks have also been used. These forms of sugar are easy to pick up by hand.
- **Sugar Packets**: A single 15 calorie serving ready to use.
- **Loaf Sugar**: The large bullet shape in which sugar was once sold.
- **Cane Syrup**: Concentrated cane juice made through a long boiling process, in which impurities are skimmed off the top.
- **Molasses**: A rich, dark byproduct of the sugar distillation process; it is available in several degrees of intensity; the darkest is called Blackstrap Molasses.
- **Sorghum Syrup**: Also known as sorghum molasses, this is similar to cane syrup, but comes from the sweet sorghum plant, a type of grass.
- **Corn Syrup**: A sweet syrup made from corn; Karo brand is the standard, with both a light (vanilla) and dark (molasses) variety.
- **HFCS**: Beginning in the 1970s, an enzyme was used with natural corn syrup to turn some of its glucose into fructose. This is the mutant horror known as High Fructose Corn Syrup. Just say no.
- **Honey**: Flower nectar and bee enzymes combine to form honey. If kept air tight and undiluted, honey will not spoil. In time, your honey may crystallize, which is absolutely fine. If you wish, you can heat and re-liquify it by zapping it twice in a microwave for 15 seconds each time. (Remove the metal lid first!). The persistence and hard work of the honey bee adds an extra kick to honey as a sweetener.

For more on sweeteners used in hoodoo, see:
"Hoodoo Herb and Root Magic" by Catherine Yronwode

A Spoonful of Sugar

Sugar, honey, and syrups of different kinds are said to "sweeten" others in the same way that they might sweeten your coffee, tea, or pancakes. This is the "Doctrine of Signatures" at its most basic.

While love drawing or reconciliation work between sweethearts may first come to mind when you think of sweetening spells, the truth is that almost any situation can do with a spoonful of sugar.

- **Home**: A peaceful home and a loving family are time-honoured reasons to begin sweetening work.
- **Court cases**: The judge, the lawyers, and the jury should all be included when sweetening a court case to go your way.
- **Bosses**: We all want the boss to have a good impression of us.
- **Co-workers**: Even worse than a single bad manager, a crowd of backstabbing "teammates" needs sweetening in the worst way.
- **Loans**: Sweetening the loan officer will help ease the way.
- **Property manager**: I've been surprised at the number of people with troublesome or even cruel landlords. Losing your home is as bad as losing a job. Make sure these people have a sweet outlook.
- **Customers**: Cinnamon sugar magic is great for bringing in clientele for any kind of business.
- **Job interviews**: Sweeten the hiring manager and bring a fixed resume to sweeten the odds.
- **Bureaucracies**: Whether an insurance claim, a hospital, or social services, every encounter with red tape is helped when you've sweetened someone to your point of view.
- **Social media:** Acquire internet friends, fans, and followers — and turn growling social media troublemakers into sweet little kittens.
- **Neighbours:** The family upstairs or on the other side of the fence will be easier to live with if their outlook is sweet and helpful.
- **Children**: The sweeter they are, the easier they are, whether frustrated toddlers or unruly teens.
- **Love**: Change disinterest to interest and friendship to romance. Keep a loving relationship alive by sweetening it regularly.
- **Reconciliation:** Turn to sugar when arguments, bitterness, or disinterest have eaten away at friendship or marriage.

Starting Simple

In hoodoo, we perform what are called "jobs" or "tricks." In order to influence others, bring good luck, or attract what we desire, we "fix" items which will be touched by our targets. Sachet powders, condition oils, and special baths and washes all have their place when laying down tricks. Incense is also a staple, used to perfume the very air with molecules of the herbs and sweeteners used in the work.

A SIMPLE POWDER TO ATTRACT POSITIVE ATTENTION

Sift confectioners sugar and powdered cinnamon to a light tan tone. This sachet will attract others to you. Use it on resumes, business cards, love letters, legal papers, official forms, greeting cards — anything you send or give to your target. Sprinkle it over the item in question, calling out the name of your target. "Customers, I reach out to you and sweeten you toward my goals." Using your three middle fingers, draw downward in a wavy "S" through the powder. Then give it several quick taps to remove the powder. You want the sugared cinnamon scent to remain, with no actual powdery traces.

A SIMPLE INCENSE FOR POSITIVE ENERGY AND INTENT

The hair from a coconut husk mixed with brown sugar may be burned on a self-lighting charcoal round to enhance any positive work. Light the charcoal on a bed of sand, then add the coconut and brown sugar mixture. You may then pass any item through the smoke, calling out your petition or desire. Socks are one favourite, whether your own or a loved one's. "Lord Jesus, sweeten my path through life" or "Lord Jesus, keep [name of loved one] coming home to me."

SMOKELESS ROOM PERFUMES

To prepare your home for a "sweet" evening, blow a bit of sachet powder into the air or boil a pot of water fixed with dash of vanilla extract and a teaspoon of sugar. To spice it up, add "pumpkin pie spice," a mix of cinnamon, ginger, cloves, allspice, and nutmeg.

For more on Powders and Incense in Hoodoo see:
LuckyMojo.com/powders.html
LuckyMojo.com/incense.html

Name-Papers and Petition-Papers

Hoodoo name-papers and petition-papers show us the import placed on the written word and the names of people. There are many styles — none of them "best" and none of them "wrong." Here is a popular way to combine a name-paper and a petition-paper on one sheet of paper.

I use pencil and torn brown paper bag paper, sometimes switching to red or green ink for love or money work. I prefer to tear a round or square piece of paper rather than use scissors to cut one out. (I try for square, and if I fail I go for round!) Write the name of the target of your work — boss, boyfriend, wife, or anyone you need to sweeten — on three different lines. (Seven and thirteen are also good numbers.) I use full names if I have them, and a generic term like "loan officer" if I don't. Adding your name is optional; to do so, turn your paper ninety degrees, and write your name (or sign your signature) on three different lines, crossing your target's name. Try not to get hung up over the colour of ink or the type of paper or the number of times you wrote something. Make your paper as nice as you can, and if you don't like it, simply start over and try again.

Around the outside of the names, in a circle, you may write out your request. Tradition says to keep your pen or pencil to the paper at all times. It can take several tries to get this part right! "Love me love me love me" is a nice choice for romance work. "Give me a raise give me a raise give me a raise" would work for your boss. The sky's the limit here.

You can also put small iconic drawings in the four corners of your petition-paper. Try hearts, dollar signs, or little houses. Give Spirit the chance to bring something appropriate to your imagination.

Hoodoo condition oils may be dabbed on the four corners and center of the paper in a quincunx or five-spot pattern, like a five on dice or a domino.

Fixing a Sugar Bowl

So let's deploy our first petition-paper, hiding it in plain sight. A sugar bowl on the table, used for coffee or tea, can be a center of sweetening for the home. A kitchen sugar canister or cookie jar can also be effective. But we need to use our petition-papers to both specify those we wish to sweeten and implore both sugar and Spirit to do as we wish.

The ideal sugar bowl for our use is not flat-bottomed, but footed, with a hidden area beneath it which we can fill as we choose. Crafty folks affix green felt across the bottom, to hide the trick from view. But how many people are going to be looking under the sugar bowl?

A SUGAR BOWL FOR PEACE IN THE HOME

Place a pinch of lavender flowers, a pinch of basil and a whole clove in the center of your paper. Fold the paper toward yourself, to bring peace toward you. Turn it ninety degrees and fold it again. Continue until you have a tight "packet" with the names far inside. Tape your packet underneath the sugar bowl and use it on the table everyday!

A SUGAR BOWL TO BRING TRUE LOVE

To turn a petition-paper into a packet for romance, add a rosebud, a piece of cinnamon stick, and a piece of cherry bark. This packet takes more skill to fold, since it is chunkier. Tie it with red thread like you'd gift wrap a present to make it easier to hide beneath your sugar bowl.

A SUGAR BOWL FOR A FAITHFUL MARRIAGE

Include a pinch of coriander seed, a pinch of cumin seed, and a single red clover flower in your packet. Women often add a sprig of rosemary. Seeds tend to roll during packet folding, so take care!

A SUGAR BOWL TRICK FOR RENEWED MARRIAGE VOW

If your spouse has left home, place your wedding ring in the sugar bowl overnight to create sweet thoughts of your marriage. This was a favourite spell taught by Susie Bosselmann of the Lucky Mojo Curio Co., whose lady-hearted phone advice was a help to so many.

Packets and sugar bowls like these have a long history in hoodoo, and many things can be found inside to augment the strength of the work.

Personal Concerns

A personal concern in hoodoo is something which is intimately linked to the target of the work. By sympathetic magic, anything done to the target's personal concerns is also done to the target.

Nail clippings, foot skin, semen, menstrual blood, hair — all are personal concerns. Dirt from the target's foot track or shoe are particularly prized. The oldest love spell in the world may be the feeding of menstrual blood to the one you love. Men can do the same trick with semen. Always say the name of your beloved as you make these recipes.

HOT CHOCOLATE AND PERSONAL CONCERNS FOR LOVE

Fix your spoon with a drop or two of your personal concerns on the tip. Combine one tablespoon each of cocoa and sugar plus a pinch of salt in a small saucepan. Add a bit of very hot water and, using your fixed spoon, mix well. Add a cup of milk and heat until warm.

TRUFFLES WITH PERSONAL CONCERNS FOR LOVE

7 green cardamom pods 1 cup heavy cream
9-10 ounces dark chocolate, shaved or chopped
2 tablespoons unsalted butter (room temperature)
Confectioners' sugar with cocoa or cinnamon for dusting

Crush the cardamom pods with a mortar and pestle. Combine heavy cream and cardamom in a saucepan. Slowly bring to a boil. Remove from heat, cover, and set aside. Melt the chocolate in a double boiler, adding your personal concerns. Strain the cream, discard cardamom, and return cream to a boil. Remove cream from heat and place in an electric mixer. Add chocolate to your cream. Beat gently to mix them. Add butter, a piece at a time, and continue to beat. When smooth, cover and refrigerate until firm. Dust a sheet of wax paper with dusting sugar. Spoon out a small ball of chilled chocolate mixture. Dust your hands and roll the chocolate ball until it is coated with dusting powder.

Don't go it alone —view a truffle making video on YouTube!

For more on personal concerns see:
LuckyMojo.com/bodyfluids.html

Harry Middleton Hyatt

An Anglican minister and folklore collector, Harry Middleton Hyatt is one reason we have such powerful documentation of hoodoo practices today. His recordings of the spiritual and magical beliefs of African-Americans resulted in a five-volume compendium called *Hoodoo - Conjuration - Witchcraft - Rootwork.*

Beginning in 1936, Hyatt used a wax cylinder recording device to capture more than 1,600 interviews with Black conjure practitioners in Alabama, Arkansas, Florida, Georgia, Illinois, Louisiana, Maryland, Mississippi, North Carolina, South Carolina, Tennessee, and Virginia. Hyatt's four-year project resulted in close to 5,000 pages of detailed spells and tricks being preserved for future study.

In addition to this massive work, Hyatt's earlier *Folklore from Adams County Illinois* covered many different cultures in one locale. He also conducted interviews in 1970 in Florida as he completed *Hoodoo - Conjuration - Witchcraft - Rootwork*, which finally saw print in the 1970s.

Hyatt's phonetic transcriptions can be difficult to read, so I have rendered these in more accessible English. The following spell, collected in Memphis, Tennessee, in 1939, came from Informant 1532, a fifty-year-old female root worker. It shows the importance of the foot track as a personal concern as well as how sugar can be used to influence a target.

SUGARING A FOOT TRACK TO KEEP A MAN YOURS

"Now, listen. If he's leaving the house and you want him to return, you catch that dirt from his toes back to the heel, pull it back. Then you take that dirt and preserve it in some kind of little can and place sugar — you know that sugar is the tamer of the world. The wildest beast, the worst beast, it will tame any of them, the sugar will. Add a little sugar in that and a little salt, and place it in a can somewhere and conceal it in a corner where it will be kept quietly, and as long as you hold that dirt from his feet, you've got him for life.

"There's two things that control an individual, two things, his name and his track."

For more on Harry M. Hyatt see:
LuckyMojo.com/hyatt.html

Sweet Baths and Sugar Scrubs

Cleansing baths are often prescribed in hoodoo for the removal of curses, jinxes, and other messes put upon one by an enemy. These baths, with their emphasis on mineral salts, can prove harsh to the skin. Sweet baths, on the other hand, have a beautiful nature all their own. Many spas now offer sugar as a gentler alternative to the salt scrub for exfoliation or removing the outer layer of dead skin cells. Sugar is a delicate abrasive.

When bathing in the conjure tradition, we bring good things up, from the feet to the top of the head, and we push bad things away, from the head down to the feet. This marks hoodoo as an earth-based tradition, rather than one focused on a sky god delivering good from above. Bathing before dawn, stepping out of the bath between two white candles, air drying while reading the Psalms, and pouring out an offering of bathwater in our yards or at a crossroads are all time-honoured traditions in hoodoo.

With these sweet baths and sugar scrubs, rinse thoroughly, until any feeling of stickiness has turned to a smooth, silky sensation.

A SIMPLE HOODOO SUGAR SCRUB FOR THE HOME

Mix one half-ounce hoodoo condition oil (the standard Lucky Mojo size) and one tablespoon of granulated sugar. You may use a little more or a little less sugar to get the right consistency. If the scrub is too powerfully scented, add another tablespoon of sugar and a tablespoon of unscented almond, olive, or coconut oil. You may also add the contents of one herbal tea bag. Lavender (for peace), hyssop (for forgiveness), rose (for romance), chamomile (for luck), and licorice (to force love) are some choices. The best thing about this sugar scrub is that it's perfect for one-time use.

A SUGAR SCRUB FOR MULTIRACIAL COUPLES

Loosely fill a wide-mouth glass jar half with white and half with brown sugar. Dump the sugar into a bowl and combine well. Slowly add oil. (Olive oil has deep roots in hoodoo, but almond oil is lighter in scent.) Add vanilla fragrance and rose petals for power. Pray as you add oil and mix, add oil and mix, add oil and mix, until you reach "scrub texture." Return the mixture to your container. Brings love to all couples, but especially when cultural differences place added stress.

A SUGARED HERB BATH TO DRAW NEW LOVE

One way to prepare an herbal bath is to boil a tea from the herbs and pour it in the bath. Another is to place a muslin sack of herbs in the bath. This makes for easy clean up, but if you like rose petals floating on the water, I say go for it! To draw new love, I recommend a tablespoon of sugar, a handful of rose petals, a handful of lavender flowers, a pinch of catnip, a handful of red clover flowers, a cardamom seed, and a stick of cinnamon. Bathe by the light of red candles.

A SUGAR BATH FOR LOVE PROTECTION

Once you've found your love, it's a good idea to work at least weekly to keep it. A tablespoon each of epsom salt, kosher salt, and sugar, plus three bay leaves will do the trick. Mix with a clockwise motion in warm to hot bath water, and recite the 23rd Psalm. Try to draw your lover's bath every once in a while — or take it together!

A SUGAR BATH TO REVERSE BAD LUCK IN LOVE

For a fresh start in the love department, use this bath once a week for thirteen weeks. Mix one half pound sugar, one pound rock salt, two ounces dill leaves, thirteen star anise pods, two ounces lemon mint, two ounces white sage, and two cups of white clover flowers.

A SUGAR BATH FOR SEDUCTION

Lightly crushed juniper berries with sugar and chopped ginger root will heat up your evening. Gay men, add safflower petals to the mix!

A SUGAR BATH TO HELP HEAL A BROKEN RELATIONSHIP

A bath of star anise, violet leaf, balm of Gilead buds, and sugar helps reconcile a couple that is arguing, on the outs, or even divorced.

A SUGAR BATH TO SWEETEN DREAMS

Hops flowers are said to drive away nightmares. A brown sugar and hops flower bath will sweeten the dreams of child or adult.

A BLUE WATER BATH FOR SUCCESS

Crush one laundry blueing square (such as Reckitt's Crown Blue brand) and mix it into your warm bath with a tablespoon each of ammonia and sugar. I like to add a dash of Florida Water cologne.

Uncrossing Sugar Bath

To be under "crossed conditions" is to have a hex, jinx, or curse on you, to have been "thrown at," "rootworked," or had a "mess" placed on you. Uncrossing baths are prescribed to remove blocked and crossed conditions, restore good luck, and overcome enemy spells.

The following four-ingredient, five-day uncrossing bath comes from the same rootworker, Hyatt's Informant 1532, we encountered earlier, and it includes Hyatt's questions as well. This woman's work is an excellent example of down-home simplicity in Southern conjure, and it is similar to other uncrossing recipes Hyatt learned while in Memphis.

> "There's another bath that I bathe. I'm telling you to take five baths in this, for five days. Now, this bath that I fix — now my best ingredient in this bath is soda [baking soda, sodium bicarbonate, a natural anti-bacterial deodorant]. And into this two tablespoons of soda I add two tablespoons of sugar, two of salt, and two of mustard powder, and that's all. Then you place this mixture in a small quantity of water, about four cups of water, let it be real warm, and then you take that and sponge your whole entire body with it, and then you rinse it off."
>
> *("In all this bathing, according to your motions, you always bathe down?")*
>
> "Down, down, like you say. If you bathe yourself down, that sugar will sweeten your body. The salt is a saving ingredient, isn't it? That mustard is for sweating possession out of you, and that soda opens the pores and dries that stuff out. And regardless of whatever may be done, whatever, you'll sure be able to come free."
>
> *("You take this bath if anybody has put a spell on you and this bath draws it out?")*
>
> "It really will, yeah, it really will. And then it'll drive enemies away and make peace in the time of confusion. Then it'll help you to be successful, to go forth into the world and accomplish what you try to accomplish. You'll find there's nothing under the sun no greater than those four little common things."

For more on bathing in the hoodoo tradition, see:
LuckyMojo.com/baths.html

Cleopatra's Beauty Secrets

For many, Cleopatra VII is the epitome of feminine strength. She used her power over men as the last pharaoh of Ancient Egypt, outlasting her father and brothers in the role. Ensnaring the hearts of Julius Caesar and Marc Antony, two of the most powerful men of her time, she presented herself to the Egyptian people as the embodiment of the goddess Isis.

Glamour, the magic of beauty, is an ancient art, and Cleopatra was certainly an admirable practitioner. The most persistent rumour about her beauty secrets is her daily use of a milk and honey bath. Honey is a humectant, attracting and retaining moisture, and its antibacterial qualities may help heal cuts, abrasions, scalds, and minor acne. The lactic acid in milk dissolves dirt, oil, and dead skin cells. Together, beyond any practical benefits, milk and honey are an indulgent pleasure for the senses.

CLEOPATRA'S LEGENDARY BEAUTY BATH

Three to four cups of raw milk and half to one cup of unfiltered honey were the only ingredients Cleopatra needed. After a full cleansing in her first tub, she was rinsed and ready for her soak. Her second tub held the milk and honey, into which warm water had been blended.

A MORE MODERN TAKE ON HONEY AND MILK

Whole powdered milk (none of this skim business) and pure honey, half a cup of each, are poured into warm running water. Soak for fifteen to twenty minutes, adding more warm water as necessary.

ADDED OATMEAL SCRUB TO SOOTHE ITCHING SKIN

Fill a muslin bag with uncooked rolled oats (not instant oatmeal!) and tie it off. Prepare a milk and honey bath as above and squeeze the oatmeal bag in the bath so the oats release their soothing essence. Scrub lightly with the muslin, which can be washed and reused.

PURE POWDER HONEY BATH

Mix two cups whole powdered milk, one cup oat flour, half a cup honey powder, two tablespoons corn starch, one quarter cup baking soda, and two tablespoons finely crushed flowers (rose, lavender, marigold or chamomile). Keep airtight. Use two to four tablespoons per bath. This one is great for gift giving.

Floor Washes to Attract Business

Sweetening customers to you makes all the sense in the world. In addition to using a sweetening sachet on business cards, the following washes will help bring customers to your door. In hoodoo, to clear off bad luck or messes, we start at the back and move toward the front, sweeping the old problems straight out the door. We will then wash up the walk and toward the door to bring good things (like money and customers) inside. Remember, we cleanse or uncross first, removing bad influences, then bring in good luck or attraction, by washing inward.

TWO-WAY BUSINESS AND PROTECTION FLOOR WASH

This two part formula begins with a cleansing wash made from one tablespoon each of oil of bergamot orange, oil of clove, and oil of cedar in a bucket of water. Mopped outwards, this will protect the premises against evildoers. The second wash is a tablespoon of oil of cinnamon, a half-handful of sugar, and your own fresh urine. Mopped inwards, this will bring you foot traffic.

TO DRAW PASSERSBY TO A STOREFRONT

Brew a tea from sassafras root, cinnamon chips, and allspice. Strain the mixture and add a tablespoon of saltpeter, a tablespoon of sugar, and a tablespoon of ammonia. Wash the sidewalk leading to the door.

TO ATTRACT CUSTOMERS TO A BROTHEL

Sprinkle sugar inside a man's left shoe and burn it to ash. Mix this ash with a tablespoon of urine, a tablespoon of sugar, and a tablespoon of salt. Urine, also called chamber lye, is an excellent personal concern, but it can be replaced with ammonia if you prefer.

NEW ORLEANS FISH FRY SIDEWALK SCRUB

Mix a tablespoon of geranium oil, a tablespoon of sugar, and a tablespoon of cinnamon into a large bucket of water. Scrub down the sidewalk with this recipe to bring paying customers to your fish fry!

QUICK CASH DOORSTEP WASH

Keep up your cash flow with a mix of brown sugar, red brick dust, and cinnamon. Add to water and scrub your doorstep inward.

Zora Neale Hurston

Zora Neale Hurston, one of the Harlem Renaissance's great writers, was also an anthropologist, and her collection of folklore and customs, *Mules and Men*, is another fine source for hoodoo spells. If you are not familiar with Hurston's *Their Eyes Were Watching God*, find a copy.

A JAR FOR SWEET WISHES

Hurston studied with Reverend Father Joe Watson, "The Frizzly Rooster." In describing his practice, she wrote, "There was one jar in the kitchen filled with honey and sugar. All the 'sweet' works were set in this jar. That is, the names and the thing desired were written on paper and thrust into this jar to stay. Already four or five hundred slips of paper had accumulated in the jar. There was another jar called the 'break up' jar. It held vinegar with some unsweetened coffee added. Papers were left in this one also."

TO MAKE PEOPLE LOVE YOU

Among the "Formulae of Hoodoo Doctors" recounted by Hurston is the following: "Take nine lumps of starch, nine of sugar, nine teaspoons of steel dust. Wet it all with Jockey Club cologne. Take nine pieces of [wide] ribbon, blue, red, or yellow. Take a dessert-spoonful and put it on a piece of ribbon and tie it in a bag. As each fold is gathered together call his name. As you wrap it with yellow thread call his name till you finish. Make nine bags and place them under a rug, behind an armoire, under a step or over a door. They will love you, give you everything they can get. Distance makes no difference. Your mind is talking to his mind and nothing beats that."

TO MAKE A TONIC

This recipe straddles the line between magical and medical herbalism. Hurston told it thus: "One quart of wine, three pinches of raw rice, three dusts of cinnamon (about one heaping teaspoon), five small pieces of the hull [rind] of pomegranate about the size of a fingernail, five tablespoons of sugar. Let it come to a boil, set one-half hour and strain. Dose: one tablespoon. (When the pomegranates are in season, gather all the hulls you can for use at other times in the year.)"

Keeping the Law at Bay

Sugar can be used to sweeten the police, district attorney, lawyers, hostile witnesses in a trial, the judge, or a jury.

TO BE FOUND INNOCENT IN A CRIMINAL CASE

Zora Neale Hurston was apprenticed to a rootworker named Dr. Duke when she learned this trick, which began with taking dirt from the graves of nine children. She wrote, "I was not permitted to do any of this because I was only a beginner ... They might kill me for my audacity." The dirt was put in a new white bowl and taken to the altar room. Three teaspoons each of sugar and sulphur were added. "Then he prayed over it, while I knelt opposite him," she wrote. "The spirits were asked to come with power more than equal to a man." She was then sent to buy a cheap set of men's underclothes, which were turned inside out and dressed with the graveyard dirt and sugar mix. Dr. Duke's client put them on right before the trial — along with brand new socks, the left one turned inside out.

TO KEEP THE LAW AWAY FROM BOOTLEGGERS

In March of 1938, Harry Middleton Hyatt interviewed Informant #872, a hoodoo woman of New Orleans, Louisiana. She told him how to make a sweet water to keep the police away: "You use white and brown sugar because your customers what come around your bootlegging joint — there's some white and some coloured — and you're doing that to draw your customers. But still the police won't come where they come. See, you make the water sweet, sweet, sweet and take a glass and put it in. Set it behind your door, and every morning take some of that water in your hand, just a little bit's enough, and sprinkle out your door three times, saying, 'In the name of the Father, Son, and Holy Ghost, let the policeman walk on, keep the policeman walking on, keep him going on,' and he won't bother you."

TO SWEETEN A JUDGE

To get a judge on your side, write his or her name nine times and place the paper with cinnamon and sugar in your left shoe. Now you have the judge under your feet and working for you.

European Grimoires and Asian Influences

Beginning in the 1930s, there was an influx of books into the occult and curio market, including titles such *The Ancient Book of Formulas*; *Legends of Incense, Herb, and Oil Magic; Terrors of the Evil Eye Exposed*; and *Mystery of the Long Lost 8th, 9th and 10th Books of Moses*. Rootworkers who ordered their spiritual supplies from mail order catalogues took a shine to these books, blending European, Asian, and Jewish folklore into hoodoo.

Here are two examples of this trend, the first from *The Master Key to Occult Secrets* by Henri Gamache and the second from John George Hohman's *Pow-Wows or the Long Lost Friend.*

PANCHA-AMRITA, A PURIFYING PRECIOUS LIQUID

This Hindu prescription is said to have purifying virtues. It is drunk before undertaking any big deal, engaging in money matters, or before setting out on any long or dangerous journey. The liquid is prepared as follows:

1 quart milk
$^{1}/_{4}$ lb. butter
$^{1}/_{4}$ lb. sugar
$^{1}/_{2}$ lb. honey

The butter is melted and mixed thoroughly with the sugar. The honey is mixed with the milk. Then the two are mixed together.

SWEET OIL FOR ANY INFLAMMATION

"Sweet oil possesses a great many valuable properties, and it is therefore advisable for every head of a family to have it at all times about the house in order that it may be applied in cases of necessity. It is a sure remedy, internally as well as externally, in all cases of inflammation in men and animals." The "sweet oil" in question is olive oil, an important ingredient in magic from pre-Biblical times.

For more on European grimoires in hoodoo, see:
LuckyMojo.com/young.html
LuckyMojo.com/powwows.html

Catherine Yronwode

Catherine Yronwode's study and practice of hoodoo led her to begin writing *Hoodoo in Theory and Practice* in 1995. Based on recollections of Oakland hoodoo pharmacies in the 1960s, where she learned from Southern rootworkers who had moved to California during World War II, and bolstered by serious scholarship, this book is available free of charge on the internet. In 2002, Yronwode published *Hoodoo Herb and Root Magic: A Materia Magica of African-American Conjure*. In 2003, she wrote 52 lessons for students, the *Hoodoo Rootwork Correspondence Course*. In 2013 she published *The Art of Hoodoo Candle Magic*. She is the co-owner of the Lucky Mojo Curio Co. with her husband, Nagasiva Yronwode.

POPSICLE STICK SUGAR MAGIC

Yronwode recounts a popular 1960s spell for friendship and love drawing. Buy a twin-stick Popsicle and share it with your friend. Collect both sticks. Write your name on your stick and your friend's name on his or her stick. Bind the sticks together with a rubber band, name sides in. Plunge them into a jar of sugar, and briskly rotate them back and forth "like a washing machine agitator," to get things going.

SUGAR PACKET OFFICE SWEETENING

This is a good one for offices that have a break room with a coffee maker and sugar packets. Grab a few packets on your way out the door. (This is one of the few times I will admit the use of fake sweeteners — grab those as well.) Once home, create a name-paper for each coworker you wish to influence. Layer the names, packets, and loose sugar in a bowl. Recite Psalms 33 and leave overnight. In the morning, dust the sugar off the packets and return them to the break room. The name-papers and sugar may be used again and again!

SYRUP, SAUCER, AND CANDLE FOR LOVE

One very old sweetening spell, Yronwode says, is "a plain white saucer in the center of which you burn a candle on the person's name, dressed with hoodoo oils and surrounded by a poured-out ring of pancake syrup or molasses. This old-fashioned method has the disadvantage of eventually drawing flies, but it is extremely easy to work on a short-term basis, say for one to three days."

Herbs and Roots

The following list covers herbs, roots, and seeds especially suitable for sweetening. It is drawn in part from *Hoodoo Herb and Root Magic*.

Do not eat or drink herbs until you have researched their toxicity.

- **Alfalfa**: To attract money, especially when seeking a loan.
- **Allspice**: For good fortune in business.
- **Althaea leaf or root**: Brings healing spirits into the home.
- **Angelica**: Added protection for children in peaceful home work.
- **Balm of Gilead buds**: To heal broken relationships.
- **Basil**: Brings happiness and money to the family.
- **Blood root**: Renews respect between family members.
- **Blue flag root**: When sweetening a boss for a raise or promotion.
- **Borage flowers**: Calming influence in any overwrought situation.
- **Calamus root**: A bit forceful, but can be used in court cases.
- **Caraway seed**: Protection for children in happy home work.
- **Cardamom seed**: Super-sexy passion herb.
- **Catnip**: "Captivate" and "capture" are the key words with catnip!
- **Cherry bark**: For sexual attraction in or out of marriage.
- **Chia seed**: To stop gossip between friends, family, or coworkers.
- **Cinnamon**: All-in-one attractant for love, luck, and money.
- **Cloves**: For friendly sweetening work and to stop gossip.
- **Coriander seed**: To bring love and faithfulness.
- **Cubeb berries**: To inspire fiery love, whether new or old.
- **Cumin seed**: To keep your lover faithful and protect the home.
- **Damiana**: Used for sexual love and lust situations.
- **Deer's tongue**: When seeking a marriage proposal or court verdict.
- **Dill leaf**: Used for those who are unlucky in love.
- **Dill seed**: Adds irresistibility to glamour work.
- **Fenugreek seed**: Will help bring money through wages or luck.
- **Flax seed**: Added protection for children in sweet home work.
- **Gentian root**: Used in love magic.
- **Ginger root**: To heat things up sexually.
- **Grains of Paradise**: Make wishes come true at home or on the job.
- **Gravel root**: When seeking a new job or increase in pay.
- **Honeysuckle flowers**: To tie your lover to you.

- **Hops flowers**: To end nightmares and sweeten dreams.
- **Hyssop**: Removes sin and helps lovers forgive.
- **Jasmine flowers**: To enhance dreams of love and romance.
- **Juniper berries**: Lower inhibitions and enhance sexuality.
- **Lavender flowers**: Bring harmony to love, platonic or romantic.
- **Lemon Mint (Bergamot Mint)**: To attract a new lover.
- **Licorice root**: A little strong, but can help change a person's mind.
- **Life Everlasting**: Promotes health in the home.
- **Little John to Chew**: The most famous court case root.
- **Lotus root**: For love and protection.
- **Lovage root**: For passion with a lover of the opposite gender.
- **Motherwort**: Brings peace to home and family.
- **Passion flower**: For peace and blessings in the home.
- **Patchouli leaf**: To attract both love and money.
- **Pennyroyal**: To bring peace and reconciliation to the family.
- **Poppy seed or flower**: Adds confusion to glamour spells.
- **Queen Elizabeth root**: Famous root to attract men.
- **Raspberry leaf**: To keep lovers from straying.
- **Red Clover flower**: For a happy and prosperous marriage.
- **Rose petal and bud**: To draw and keep true love.
- **Rosemary**: Strengthens and protects women in the home.
- **Safflower petal**: Used by gay men to attract a dominant partner.
- **Sarsaparilla root**: Brings health, blessings, money and passion.
- **Sassafras root**: To make your money last longer.
- **Senna leaf**: To get love from one who doesn't notice you.
- **Skullcap**: To encourage fidelity.
- **Slippery Elm bark**: To stop gossip when sweetening others.
- **Solomon's seal root**: Sweeten teachers and attract good grades.
- **Spikenard**: Love herb mentioned in The Bible.
- **Star Anise**: For good luck and psychic vision.
- **Sumac berry**: For a better result in court cases.
- **Thyme**: Sweetens dreams and attracts health and money.
- **Tonka bean**: Makes love wishes come true.
- **Vanilla bean:** Placed in the sugar bowl at table, for love.
- **Violet leaf**: To attract love, new or old.
- **White Clover flower**: To purify and protect.
- **White Sage**: Brings wisdom and clears negative energy.

Herbal Mixtures

Once you know the traditional uses of the most popular hoodoo herbs, they can be mixed and matched to create suitable combinations for any situation where sweetening is desired.

If the herbs are edible, you can make a tea of them and add sugar, honey, and other ingredients for a refreshing beverage.

To bathe with herbal mixtures, place them loose in a muslin bag and add the bag to a regular honey and milk bath.

To work with these herbal blends in name- or petition-paper packets, crush them very fine and sprinkle them into the papers from which you fold the petition-packets that you place in sugar or honey jar spells.

Herbs are your spirit-allies — befriend them and they will open many doors for you and bring about improved conditions in your life.

- **Reconciliation**: Hyssop, balm of Gilead buds, rose buds or petals, althaea leaf, and lavender.
- **Happy boss**: Blue flag root, gravel root, and allspice.
- **Fiery kisses**: Ginger root, juniper berries, catnip, cubeb berries, cinnamon, cardamom, and rose petals.
- **A sweet new love**: Damiana, violet leaf, lemon mint. cubeb berries, catnip, and jasmine flowers.
- **Peaceful home**: Motherwort, pennyroyal, flax seed, lavender, angelica, borage flowers, rosemary, and althaea.
- **Sweeten the teacher**: Solomon's seal, sage, and bay laurel leaf.
- **Special sex sugar**: Vanilla bean, rose petals, whole cloves, star anise, and cardamom pods.
- **Sympathetic judge and jury**: Little John to Chew, slippery elm, licorice root, and sumac berries.
- **To get a loan or other financial request granted:** Five finger grass, fenugreek seed, and licorice root.
- **For faithfulness:** Skullcap, raspberry leaves, honeysuckle flowers, white clover flowers.

For more on herb and roots used in hoodoo see:
"Hoodoo Herb and Root Magic" by Catherine Yronwode
Herb-Magic.com

Hoodoo Foods

Each year, Sister Robin Petersen of the Lucky Mojo Curio Co. hosts an event in which the Ladies' Auxiliary of Missionary Independent Spiritual Church competes with magical recipes to enchant the palate and bewitch the brain. The collected entries are published in the *Hoodoo Food! Conjure Cook-Off and Rootwork Recipe Round-Up*. Here are a few of my favourites.

CELTIC SCOTTISH HARMONIOUS OFFICE SHORTBREAD

$1\frac{1}{3}$ cups butter, about $2\frac{1}{2}$ sticks (an emollient))
$\frac{2}{3}$ cup sugar (for sweetening people and for goodwill)
$\frac{3}{4}$ teaspoon salt (for protection)
$\frac{3}{4}$ teaspoon vanilla (for loving kindness and luck)
$\frac{1}{2}$ teaspoon allspice (for money luck and to relax the mind)
$\frac{1}{2}$ teaspoon cloves (for friendship, to stop gossip, and for luck)
$\frac{1}{2}$ teaspoon cinnamon (for money and for success in business)
$\frac{1}{4}$ teaspoon nutmeg (for money in business)
$3\frac{1}{3}$ cups flour

Cream butter and sugar in a bowl, by hand. Add salt, vanilla, and spices, then cream again. Add flour 1 cup at a time, mixing by hand while reciting Psalms 133: "Behold, how good and how pleasant it is for brothers to dwell together in unity!"

Butter 4 pie tins, make dough into 4 big balls, and push each ball into its pan with your fingers. Cover the whole tin, even up the sides. Use the palm of your hand to flatten and your finger to press the sides to make nice pie ridges. Use a fork to prick the flattened dough all over, making nice little rows. See all the mean go away and fill in with nice and calm. Make holes everywhere.

Bake at 375°F 'til golden — about 10-15 minutes — or longer if needed. Once out of the oven, immediately cut like pizza, making 6 long cuts across as you turn the tins. You can do squares instead, if you want. While still hot, sprinkle sugar all over the top while reciting Psalms 4:8: "I will lie down and sleep in peace, for you alone, O Lord, make me dwell in safety." Cool, then put in a festive tin or container with wax paper lining. Share with office co-workers for friendship, harmony, and prosperity on the job.

— Danette Wilson

KISS ME NOW BALLS

1 1/2 cup butter
2 tablespoon molasses (a love-sweetener)
3/4 cup brown sugar (a love-sweetener)
3 cups all-purpose flour
1 teaspoon ground ginger (to hurry and heat up a relationship)
1/2 teaspoon ground nutmeg (increase the odds in your favour)
1/2 teaspoon ground cinnamon (luck and money, heating up love)
1/4 teaspoon damiana (sexual potency; an aphrodisiac)
1/4 teaspoon catnip (enticing sexuality and flirtation)
1/4 teaspoon cardamom (to attract a lover)
1/4 teaspoon allspice (money-luck, release of mental tension)
1/4 teaspoon ground or crushed cubeb (to attract a lover)
1 tablespoon flaxseed meal (health and well-being)
1 teaspoon vanilla extract (love and romance)
1 tablespoon water (spiritual cleansing)
1/4 teaspoon menstrual blood or other sexual fluid (love-binding)
1 cup chopped pecans or other nuts (male sexual potency)
1 coon dong or 1 whole Queen Elizabeth root (optional)
1/2 cup confectioners' sugar

Grind your cubebs, damiana, and catnip in a mortar and pestle, also prepare your chopped nuts. Stir together the flour, spices, and flaxseed meal. (For extra kick: To attract a man, stir the dry ingredients with a Coon Dong; to attract a woman, place the dry ingredients in a closed container and shake them up with a whole Queen Elizabeth root. Pray fervently for your desire while doing so.)

Cream together the butter, molasses, and sugar, then stir in vanilla, water, and sexual fluids. Add the flour mixture and nuts, stirring as you go. Mix until blended. Some people cover and chill the dough for three hours at this point, but except on the hottest days, this is not strictly necessary. Preheat your oven to 325° F.

Shape the dough into small balls. Place on an ungreased cookie sheet and bake for 15 to 20 minutes. Remove from pan to cool on wire racks. When cool, roll in confectioners' sugar. Store at room temperature in an airtight container. Makes about 4 dozen.

— Miss Michaele Maurer

LOVE MUFFINS WITH ROSE GLAZE

½ cup dried rose hips, cleaned, de-seeded, and cut
1 large sweet red or pink apple, cored and grated
2 cups all purpose flour
½ cup sugar
1 tablespoon baking powder
½ teaspoon salt
1 teaspoon ground ginger
¼ teaspoon ground cardamom
1 egg, beaten
1 cup milk
¼ cup butter, melted
¼ cup honey

Preheat oven to 400 degrees. Lightly butter muffin pan, or insert paper liners. Mix grated apple and rose hips, and set aside. Combine the flour, sugar, baking powder, salt, ginger, and cardamom, and mix well. In a separate bowl, blend the egg, milk, melted butter, and honey. (Measure ¼ cup butter in a 1 cup measuring cup, then add honey until the total is ½ cup. The butter makes it easy to get the honey out of the cup.) You may add your personal concerns. Mix the dry ingredients into the wet stirring as you go. The batter will be lumpy. Fold in the apple and rose hips mix. Fill the muffin cups ³/₄ full and bake for 20-25 minutes, until the tops are lightly browned and the edges begin to pull away. Let cool a few minutes in the pan, then turn out onto a rack to finish cooling. Makes twelve muffins.

Glaze:
1 cup confectioner's powdered sugar
1-2 tablespoons rose water
Red food colouring (optional)

Place powdered sugar in a bowl. Stir in rose water a few drops at a time. To test glaze thickness, lift the spoon: glaze that drips into the bowl should leave a visible surface trail before sinking back in. If glaze is too thick, add a drop of rose water; if too thin, add powdered sugar. Using a toothpick, pick up a drop of food colouring, and stir it into the glaze. For a darker shade, repeat. Arrange cooled muffins on a rack in a tray and drizzle with glaze. Allow the glaze to dry.

Rose hips, apple, and rose water promote love, cardamom incites lust, and ginger heats things up! Sugar and honey sweeten your intended toward you, and butter "butters them up."

— Carin Huber

LUCKY MONEY MARRIAGE BERRIES

4 cups fresh raspberries (female love and sexuality, the womb)
½ cup sour cream (the fat of the milk)
¼ cup half and half (the thin with the thick)
3 tablespoons brown sugar, lightly packed (love's dark sweetness)
½ teaspoon cinnamon (for a wealthy husband; money luck)
½ teaspoon orange extract (orange flowers symbolize marriage)

Reserve berries. Mix other ingredients in the order given, stirring well. Chill one hour. Place berries in individual bowls. Drizzle sauce over berries.

— Gabrielle Davis

HONEY CAKE TO SWEETEN BUSINESS ASSOCIATES

½ cup butter (a social lubricant)
1 ½ cups sugar (for sweetness)
1 cup honey (for more sweetness)
4 eggs (for new beginnings; it is a traditional New Year's cake)
1 cup strong, unadulterated, cold coffee (to wake up their attention)
4 cups flour (well, it is a cake, after all!)
1 teaspoon baking soda (to make the money rise)
1 teaspoon baking powder (to make the money rise still faster)
½ teaspoon fresh-grated nutmeg powder (for money luck)
½ teaspoon cinnamon powder (for more money luck)
½ teaspoon allspice powder (for even more money luck)
½ teaspoon ginger powder (to heat them up to act on your behalf)

Cream butter and sugar, pour in honey, stir well, beat in eggs, stir in coffee, set aside. In another bowl, sift flour with baking soda, baking powder, and spices. Blend dry mix into liquid. Bake in a greased bread pan one hour at 350 degrees. This Honey Cake of Rosh Hashanah (Jewish New Year) is from my grandmother Ida Kohn Erlanger, whose family were bankers in Nuremberg. My mother's cousin Max Reizenstein, son of Lina Kohn Reizenstein (Ida's sister), also had this recipe. After fleeing Nazi Germany, he bought a bakery in Auckland, New Zealand and sold Honey Cakes worldwide. The Kohn family Honey Cake always brings money!

— Catherine Yronwode

Red Apples and Sweet Onions

Vibrant colour and sweet taste make red apples and onions traditional for sweetening. The onion has more "bite" than the apple, for stubborn targets.

APPLE AND ONION SOUP FOR LOVE

1 tablespoon butter
1 lb. medium red onions, thinly sliced (for love and luck)
1/2 lb. medium red apples, diced (for love)
6 cups chicken, beef, or vegetable broth
Personal concerns, if desired (to link the work to yourself)
1 pinch salt (protection)
1 pinch black pepper (protection)
1/2 cup grated Swiss or Gouda cheese
1/2 cup croutons
3 tablespoons fresh basil, chopped very fine (for a happy home)

Melt butter in a pot over medium heat. Add onions and apples. Sauté until apples and onions are tender. Add broth. Partially cover, and simmer 30 minutes, stirring occasionally. Add salt and pepper to taste. To serve, ladle hot soup over cheese in individual bowls, garnish with croutons and a chiffonade of basil. Serves 6.

A RED APPLE TIN TO SWEETEN A FIGHTING COUPLE

Write a petition-paper no taller than the red apple, which is first cored. Roll the paper tightly, place it in the apple, and allow it to unfurl within. Put the apple in a metal coffee tin. Mix the sweetener of your choice with cinnamon, and cover the apple with this while reciting scripture or your wish. To deploy your apple tin, bury it in the yard of the couple whose relationship you wish to "fix."

A FIXED RED ONION FOR A LOVING HOME

Prepare an appropriately sized petition-paper to fit within a cored sweet red onion. Place in a flower pot, fill with sweetener and cinnamon and cover with potting soil. Plant a fern to protect the home, lavender for love, or rosemary for a woman's strength. Makes a great gift, and hides your work from others.

Container Spells

In the previous spells, apples and onions were used as containers for sweeteners, herbs, and petition-papers. Gourds, tins, boxes, clay pots, glass bottles, and jars in an endless variety of colours, shapes, and sizes are also used. They can even be painted to give added expression to your work.

A SIMPLE SUGAR BOX SPELL FOR LOVE

Place a photo of the person you desire face up in a cigar, pencil, or other shallow box. Cover the photo completely in granulated sugar. Draw a heart shape into the sugar and close the box. Keep hidden away on a high shelf or tucked beneath a chest of drawers. When you wish to give an extra jolt of sweetness, shake the box back and forth, until the heart is gone, redrawing it anew in the pristine sugar.

A SUGAR SHAKER TO EXCITE PASSION

Place an appropriately sized petition-paper within a bottle, with your writing facing inward. Fill with granulated sugar. Add seven juniper berries. Seal and shake when physical romance is desired.

A SUGAR KEY TO SWEETEN TIME IN JAIL

If you have a loved one in jail, this trick will help their stay be briefer and easier. Paste their photo on a wide-rimmed jar. Fill with granulated sugar. Get a skeleton key and shove it straight into the sugar, like a key in a lock. Turn the key daily and recite Psalms 23.

SWEET CITRUS FOR BUSINESS LUCK AT A BAD LOCATION

There are certain locations that are just bad for business. Within a year, every new business that opens its doors in these locations just shuts down for good. To sweeten the situation and turn that luck around, you will need two large pots, two citrus plants, two halved lemons, two thin cardboard boxes, a bag of soil, and a bag of sugar. Hand copy Psalms 108 twice. Place one into each box, along with both halves of a lemon. Pour sugar over the lemon halves, reciting the appropriate adage ("When life gives you lemons..."). Close each box, and place into a pot. Plant the citrus plants in the pots and set them out invitingly on either side of the front door. If your climate is too cold for citrus, use dwarf golden cypress bushes.

A recipe for dessert and a recipe for a hoodoo spell have a lot in common. A list of ingredients, a preparation methodology, an overall tone or theme. As in cooking, we know what blends well together, and we select our ingredients accordingly.

Hoodoo is not lavish. Remember what we learned about salt, sugar, mustard, and soda: "You'll find there's nothing under the sun no greater than those four little common things."

Miss Bri, a Texas reader and rootworker for many years, teaches this pleasingly pink bottle spell for love. It uses a variety of herbs, as well as hoodoo condition oils and incense from the Lucky Mojo Curio Co.

MESSAGE IN A BOTTLE

1 glass bottle or jar
Petition (can be photograph or name-paper)
Love Me Oil
Dixie Love Oil and Incense powder
Come to Me or Kiss Me Now! Oil
Sugar
Cinnamon stick
Dried red rose petals
Dried lavender
Dried cubeb berries
Dried damiana
Cardamom seeds

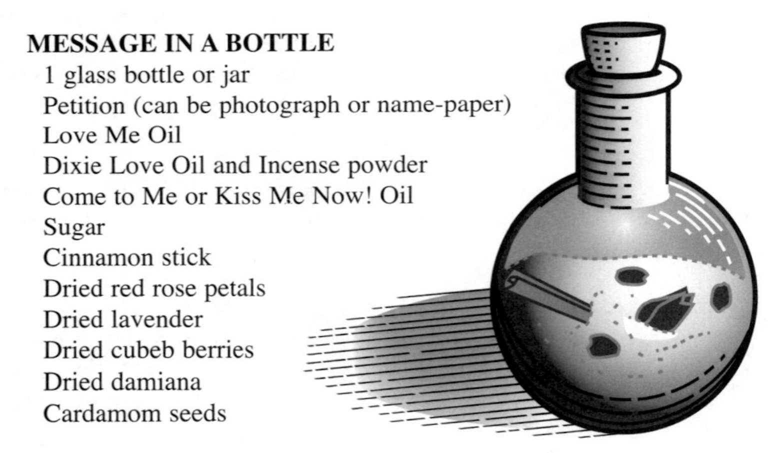

Write out a name-paper and anoint it with a blend of the three oils. Mix the sugar with the rose petals, lavender, cubeb berries, damiana, and cardamom seeds. Add the Dixie Love Incense powder to the blend, lightly anoint the cinnamon stick with the oils, and then stir the blend with the cinnamon stick clockwise, praying for your romantic desire to come to fruition as you do so.

Pour the contents into your bottle or jar, add the cinnamon stick and your name-paper. Shake the bottle as you speak out loud your prayers and romantic desires. Repeat as often as you like.

For more on container spells see:
"The Black Folder" edited by Catherine Yronwode

A Candle to Light Your Way

Oil lamps played a part in hoodoo from the beginning, but the 20th century introduction of candles, particularly odourless paraffin in a variety of colours, gave the element of fire a stronger place in rootwork, augmenting hoodoo's foundational focus on the element of earth.

The burning candle represents an emanation of prayer and the calling forth of Spirit to light our path. A plain white candle is deeply powerful and effective, and white remains our "default" colour — but a coloured candle (such as green for money, pink for friendship, or red for sexuality) adds a layer of meaning to your work.

The use of hoodoo condition oils to anoint candles adds scent and herbal evocation to the work. As in hoodoo bathing, when we oil a candle we pull the good toward us and stroke the bad away. Dusting an oiled candle with a sachet powder, such as the cinnamon powdered sugar described earlier, is a nicely old-fashioned way of working.

Because sugar does burn, it is important to watch over work that involves a plain candle touching sugar, just to be on the safe side.

A SIMPLE SUGAR BOX AND CANDLE SPELL

Buy a one-pound box of sugar. Lay it flat, and with a box cutter, knife, or scalpel, cut a heart, circle, or square in the front of the box. (I start by trying to cut a heart. If I fail, I try to save it by making a circle, using a square or rectangle as my last resort.) Deep into the sugar, poke your petition-paper or a photo of those you wish to work. Oil a candle with an appropriate condition oil and stand it straight up in the center. Pray over the work and light the candle.

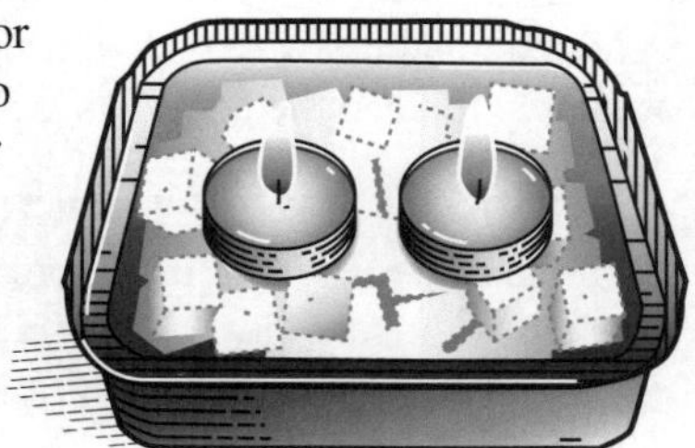

SUGAR CUBES AND TEA LIGHTS

Dr. Johannes, trained in both hoodoo and the Scandinavian folk magic tradition of trolldom, offers his variation on a sugar box: Place a petition paper beneath a stack of sugar cubes in a rectangular tinfoil pan. Position two pink tea lights on top to represent the people to be sweetened. Tea lights do not drip, and the sugar can be used later as food.

RED, WHITE, AND BLUE RETURN TO ME CANDLE

The Gifted Medium of New Orleans, Hyatt's Informant 1559, gives us this spell. A petition-paper is put under a white plate, upon which is placed a lighted candle. "Then they will place sugar and place raisins and then place steel dust. You will contact the person by calling the individual which would be in a spiritual form at the hours of nine, three, and six." Use red, white and blue candles in succession. The raisins, sugar, and steel dust also suggest red, white, and blue.

NINE WHITE LIGHTS TO GET A JOB BACK

In order to get rehired by a white individual, the Gifted Medium says to use a clear jar of powdered sugar with powdered cloves and allspice, and a name-paper. "Then there is nine white lights that must be burned upon this jar for nine successive days. And I will say unto the Sacred Heart, 'Please soften [the boss's] heart that he will give such-and-such-a-one his job back again.'"

Catholic rootworkers introduced glass-encased religious candles to hoodoo. Non-Catholics responded by designing secular glass-encased "vigil" lights. Either style of glass candle may be "fixed" with condition oils, herbs, curios, and a graphic label. When a vigil or religious light is placed on top of a person's photo, it is called "burning a candle on him" (or her) or "setting lights." Spiritual devotees may use a glass-encased light as a regular devotional offering, as a special request for intercession, or simply to keep the good work going on.

ADDING A SWEET TOUCH TO YOUR VIGIL CANDLE

In the same way that many practitioners use glitter to finish off their glass-encased candles, I will use a small sprinkle of coloured sugar or tiny bakers' decorations in the shape of hearts or flowers.

TRAVELLING WITH YOUR WEEKLY DEVOTION

It's hard to keep up a daily or weekly candle devotion when on the road. A box of birthday candles and roll of Lifesaver candies to hold them will let you sweetly offer a prayer wherever you may be.

For more on candle magic in hoodoo see:
"The Art of Hoodoo Candle Magic" by Catherine Yronwode

The Honey Jar Spell

Whether due to the "hide in plain sight" aspect of a jar of honey, the "eternal" nature of honey as non-spoiling, or this spell-family's strong rate of success, the honey jar or honey pot may be the most-tried hoodoo spell of all. I encourage clients to do it themselves because it is pure, positive magic. As such, there is nothing that can "go wrong."

Honey jars are slow and steady, perfect to keep up for a lifetime. But if you are trying to sweeten someone to you and they just will not budge, it is important that you set a time limit on the work. Your life is too important to put on hold for anyone. If the two of you are "meant to be," then God will arrange another opportunity for you down the line. In the meantime, let go, work on yourself, and allow the universe to provide the perfect love for you — perhaps with someone you've never even met!

The classic honey jar requires a petition-paper, a jar, and honey, plus a candle, personal concerns, herbs, and oils if you wish. Of course, you may use molasses, maple, Karo, or any syrup; all are equally traditional. Water plus sweeteners will ferment, causing a jar to explode, so do not add any water. Because the size of the jar is immaterial, the mini honey jar spells sold by the Lucky Mojo Curio Co. are just right, and very convenient.

A HONEY JAR SPELL FOR LOVE

Write your name-and-petition-paper, and place in it one hair from each of you, tied in a knot if possible, along with any herbs you may select. Dot the petition with a love oil and complete the folding ritual. Since all herbs are tucked away in your packet, the honey remains pure for later use in love-cookery. Press the packet into the honey with your finger. Lick your finger, saying, "As this honey is sweet on the tongue, so shall [name] be sweet on me!" Press the packet down two more times, toward the bottom of the jar, repeating the phrase. The packet may float up, but that's not important. Close the jar. Anoint a pink or red candle and burn it on the jar each Monday, Wednesday, and Friday. As wax drips down to cover your jar, you may let it build, engaging in candle wax divination if you are so gifted.

To learn about candle wax divination, see:
LuckyMojo.com/candlemagicdivination.html

A CINNAMON STICK VALENTINE

As a practicing rootworker, I find that most people cannot provide personal concerns. I make a Valentine from their names and photo, wrapping it around a cinnamon stick and tying it with red thread. Depending on which herbs I choose, I may like the look of them loose in the honey. In this case, I put all my ingredients (including two Necco Conversation Hearts) straight into the jar and pour the honey on top. Some herbs I use are toxic, so I do not eat this honey.

A HONEY JAR FOR PEACE WITHIN A GROUP

Whether it is extended family, a bickering church council, or a difficult work environment, a honey jar is an excellent choice to bring peace to any group. List every name on one petition or on many tiny papers separately. While it can be hard to provide a hair from each person, using Scotch tape on a favourite chair back may surprise you.

A HONEY JAR FOR THE TEACHER

Children excel when their teachers take a sweet and loving interest. I know one mother who kept a honey jar for each child high in her pantry, adding new teachers each year. No candles, no muss, no fuss!

A LOVING FATHER FOR YOUR CHILD

Many a single mother has found herself cursing the no-good man who won't support his child. Sweetening the situation will help a man *want* to take care of his family. Catherine Yronwode has a special petition-paper for such cases. "Use the mama and the daddy names written nine times each, side by side in two columns (because they are no longer a couple) and the baby name crossed over both, holding them all together. Then, around and around the names write: 'We are family, forever and in all ways, and let no one put this family asunder.'" In the corners of the paper, she draws four eye-shapes, just the outlines, with no pupils in the centers. Inside each eye-shape is a heart and inside each heart a dollar sign. "The meaning of this symbol in each corner is *God is watching you* (the eye shape) — *so love the child* (the heart) *and pay the money* (the dollar sign).

For more on honey jar spells see:

LuckyMojo.com/honeyjar.html

Oils to Use with Sweetening Spells

One of the most common hoodoo practices is the use of "condition oils" to consecrate just about anything. On the body, anointing oils are not merely attractive scents, but also carry purpose and intent. On the altar, dressing oils help empower objects such as lodestones, mojo bags, and candles. This is certainly the case with the traditional honey jar spell.

When burning a candle atop a honey jar, most practitioners choose to dress the candle with a condition oil. Often name-papers or photos are also dabbed with oil before being placed in the honey. While the enthusiastic may want to add an oil (or three or seven) directly to the honey in the jar, I encourage you to refrain. Use the oil on papers and candles.

Likewise, do not overdo it when adding oils to glass-encased vigil lights. If you aim for a drop or two, you may get a few extra — and, believe me, that is plenty! Too much oil can flare up, or it can drown the candle wick.

I select from the following list of Lucky Mojo brand conjure oils, often relying on Spirit to guide me. These oils (except for Special Oil No. 20) all contain herbs which can clearly be seen in the bottles.

- **Adam and Eve Oil**: To bring a "perfect" mate. Sometimes used with penis and vulva figural candles, this oil can create a physical bond difficult to break, or attract a lover "fated" in the stars.
- **Attraction Oil**: If the one you love doesn't seem to know you exist, this will do the trick! Great with lodestone spells.
- **Bewitching Oil**: Gives an extra "glamour" to your work and increases confidence in those who need a boost in self-esteem.
- **Boss Fix Oil**: When sweetening your boss seems very slow or even ineffective, this oil can kick it up a notch.
- **Chuparrosa Oil**: The hummingbird is a traditional god of love for natives from Central and North America, sucking dishonesty from the flower of your love.
- **Cleo May Oil**: Based on an old perfume formula from the 1920s, this oil is used by working girls to sweeten their clients.
- **Come To Me Oil**: To turn an acquaintance into a friend or a friend into something more!
- **Court Case Oil**: Excellent when sweetening a judge, jury, and lawyers to take your side in a civil or criminal proceeding.

- **Crucible of Courage Oil**: Adds "backbone" when the one you want faces obstacles such as race, religion, family, or a current relationship.
- **Dixie Love Oil**: A Southern recipe for down-home love, this is a good choice when starting a honey jar or other love work.
- **Fire of Love Oil**: When you need to spice up your relationship or inspire a little passion, ignite the Flames of Love.
- **Kiss Me Now! Oil**: Get past the first hurdle and go in for the lip lock. Don't just grab that kiss: make it memorable!
- **Lavender Love Drops Oil**: I was lucky to help Miss Cat finalize the formula for this same-sex relationship oil.
- **Love Me Oil**: I read First Corinthians 13 aloud when I use this old-time favourite, all-purpose love oil.
- **Marriage Oil**: Used on bride and groom candles (or their gay equivalents) or on a petition-paper to bless a current marriage or to call forth a proposal from your beloved.
- **Peaceful Home Oil**: To soothe and quiet a restless household. Good with sullen teenagers, nasty in-laws, and argumentative spouses: or when general anxiety strikes.
- **Q Oil**: The original in-the-closet oil for men and women of the "Q" persuasion, who added it in a bath of safflower petals for extra oomph. Still works wonders in this more enlightened time.
- **Reconciliation Oil**: If your marriage is on the rocks, your engagement is broken off, or you've argued once too many times with the one you love, I cannot recommend this highly enough.
- **Return To Me Oil**: It's hard to make any relationship work when geography intervenes. A good oil for reestablishing contact.
- **Special Oil No. 20**: This all-purpose oil is extremely powerful and was the original choice for honey jar spells of all kinds.
- **Stay At Home Oil**: Tired of your loved one going out on the town? That time and attention can be yours instead! This oil keeps folks home when their worst "unfaithfulness" is nothing more serious than going bowling with the guys or shopping with the gals
- **Stay With Me Oil**: Suspect an affair of the heart? Prevent divorce and keep those interested glances from turning into something more.

For more on the history and use of Hoodoo Condition Oils see: **LuckyMojo.com/oils.html**

Honey Jars on Your Altar

A honey jar on its own is just fine, but it can also serve as a candle holder in another work, such as a lodestone or moving candle spell.

FIGURAL CANDLES ATOP YOUR HONEY JAR

Figural candles are available in many shapes, from sexual organs (for generating lust) to little married couples (for a proposal or blessing a marriage). I like the little Adam and Eve naked man and woman figurals, tied together to bind the lovers to each other.

PETITIONING A SAINT FOR YOUR HONEY JAR

A triangular shape is often used when working on the altar. When calling on Saint Anthony to return a lost love, for instance, you may form a triangle with a glass of water (to quench his thirst) at the front left of the triangle, a candle at the middle rear, and a Saint Anthony statue at the front right. The honey jar is a perfect stand for the candle.

A MOVING CANDLE SPELL

The moving candle spell is a very powerful worker of change. To begin you will individually baptize one candle for each party. Hold the first candle in your left hand, and make the sign of the cross over it with your right hand, saying, "[Name] you are, and [Name] to me, you will always be." Repeat with the second candle. Now that the candles are representatives of the people in question, they are set a ways apart upon the altar, with the honey jar and a couple-candle at the center, as the "goal" to be reached. Each day the candles are lit and moved another bit toward one another, until they join in the middle. There, you will let them melt together in front of your honey jar and become one.

SEVEN-DAY LODESTONE LOVE SPELL

Begin with a pair of lodestones to represent those you wish to bring together. Male lodestones are pointed, while female lodestones are rounder in shape. Put them together in multiple arrangements until you see how they most powerfully attract. Place the lodestones on a non-metal tray (to hold any magnetic sand which may fall) seven to twelve inches apart, with their most powerful ends facing each other. Baptize the lodestones as you did with the candles in the moving candle spell and add any personal concerns you may possess. Set your honey jar behind and between, to form the apex of a triangle.

Each day, dress your honey jar candle with love-drawing oil, adding a drop to each lodestone. You will also "feed" the lodestones a little magnetic sand or anvil dust daily. Light the candle on your honey jar and read aloud from the Song of Solomon (by far the lustiest book of the Bible). At the end of the seven days, your lodestones should be touching, covered with magnetic sand. Keep them together in a safe place, renewing them from time to time.

TRIPLE GREEN MONEY SPELL

If your honey jar is for your boss, a loan officer, a new job, or to attract customers, use a green seven-knob wishing candle on top, plus a green devil figural candle and a green pyramid figural candle in front and to either side, forming a triangle. On each candle, use a different money-drawing oil. Each day for a week, light the candles and read Psalms 5. When that day's "knot" upon your honey jar is complete, snuff out your candles and await the following day. This is especially good for "training" money. Write $$¢¢$$ in each corner of the bills you wish to train, then use the money to buy job related items or hide it for others to find, increasing their blessings.

For more on the history and use of lodestones see:
LuckyMojo.com/lodestone.html

For more love spells see:
LuckyMojo.com/lovespells.html

For more money spells see:
LuckyMojo.com/moneyspells.html

Deployment, Dispersal, and Disposal

And so our spellwork is done. What next?

Deployment means to set a spell working out where someone will contact it (think of the way armies deploy troops). In hoodoo, with its emphasis on foot track magic, we want someone to walk over or near the spell, so we call deployment "laying your trick." A honey jar to attract tenants may be laid beneath the building, a sugar jar for business success may be down inside a potted plant by the front door of the store, and to keep family members home you can bury your honey pot in the backyard.

Dispersal means to send something out in all directions (think of the way the wind disperses dandelion seeds). We may want a love spell to go out into the world because we don't know where our target is. We can place it at a crossroads and ask that all who drive by carry a bit of its energy to him. We can take the work to an ant hill and open any containers, allowing the ants to communicate the magic to their brother and sister ants around the world. If there was a special relative dear to you, who always had your best interests at heart, you can bury your spell by their graveside, with a beautiful plant on top and ask their spirit to carry the work into the world.

When we dispose of a spell, we are through with it. It may have failed, we may have changed our minds about the situation, or we may have chosen a different form of spell-work. There are many ways to dispose of spells; for sweet works running water is the easiest. Not the sink or bathtub, but a stream, river, or the ocean! If your spell was in a container, open it up and gently scoop out the contents into the water. When the container is washed clean, turn and walk away, never to look back.

For more on laying tricks and disposing of ritual remains, see:
LuckyMojo.com/layingtricks.html

"You Can Catch More Flies with Honey..."

Sweetening will often do the trick when nothing else will. God calls us to love our neighbours as ourselves and to turn the other cheek toward our enemies. This does not mean that kind or just work is the first thing our human hearts desire — but when all the cursing, coercion, and hot footing are over and done, we can still turn our weary souls to sweetening. The high road may not be our first choice, but we can always make it our last.

Frequently Asked Questions

The Lucky Mojo Forum, begun in 2009, averages sixty posts a day. It is organized into four sections: technical issues, Lucky Mojo spiritual supplies by form, spiritual conditions by type, and outreach to the hoodoo community (readers, rootworkers, radio shows, workshops, and so forth).

Anyone can join the forum and ask questions about hoodoo in general or about Lucky Mojo spiritual supplies. At the forum, a dedicated crew of moderators offer hands-on wisdom daily, dishing out spells, encouragement, and advice on the vicissitudes of life — fulfilling the role of the rootworker since hoodoo's earliest days. In addition to the "mods," plenty of regular forum visitors also chime in with answers to questions, many of them presented from a background of personal experience.

All of the forum moderators are graduates of Catherine Yronwode's course, and are compensated for their time in Lucky Mojo products. Some are also professional conjure doctors, and of those, several are members of the Association of Independent Readers and Rootworkers (AIRR).

The most populated thread in the forum is that devoted to sweetening spells. No other topic comes close. At this writing, the honey and sugar spell thread holds more than 3,500 posts and has had half a million views.

The Frequently Asked Questions — and answers — that follow have been selected from the thousands of forum posts about sugar and honey spells. Here you will find answers to some of the most commonly asked and intriguing questions in the forum.

But first, here is some information about who is answering the questions:

User-names followed by an (M) are people who are or were at one time forum moderators. Those whose names are marked (M, AIRR) are moderators who are also professional members of AIRR:

Catherine Yronwode
ConjureMan Ali
Deacon Millett
Devi Spring
Dr. Johannes
Lukianos
Miss Bri
Miss Michaele

You can reach these AIRR members for readings, rootwork, magical coaching, or other professional spiritual services, at the AIRR web site:

ReadersAndRootworkers.org

• Can I use sugar water in a sweetening jar?

I was curious if you could use a jar filled with water and some sugar instead of pure honey. Does it make any difference?

— heartk0re

Yes, it makes a difference. Water plus sugar equals fermentation — you will ferment or brew some kind of fizzy alcoholic soda-beverage.

There are traditions in any system of folk magic that are taught from one person to another, and cannot be improvised from reading on the internet. If you want to eliminate the trial and error of brewing beer by mistake and see how a real honey jar spell is made, you can order any of our wonderful Lucky Mojo Honey Jar Kits.

— catherineyronwode (M, AIRR)

• Can I use a honey jar to sweeten my co-workers?

I'm well aware that a honey jar is typically used on a lover or on a person to "sweeten" them to you. My question is: Can I use it to sweeten up my co-workers to me? All six of them, including my boss?

If yes, what herbs should I use? What anointing oil for the candle?

I realize this is highly unusual for a honey jar so thanks for the help.

— Bea

Your idea of a honey jar is altogether too limited.

Basically, you are just flat *wrong*. It is not "highly unusual" to use a honey jar to sweeten co-workers, juries, bosses, teachers, loan officers, landlords, renters, and pretty much anyone, either singly or in groups.

Also, you seem to think that 1) you must use honey; 2) you must light a candle; and 3) you must add herbs or oils.

Wrong again — all of those ideas are simply options. You can make a sweet jar in a sugar bowl (no honey) with two popsicle sticks (no candle, no oil). You can make a honey spell in an Apple (no jar) and plant a tree on it (no candle, no oil). You can make a sugar spell in a sugar packet (no honey and no jar) and sneak it into someone's tea (no candle, no oil).

No need to re-invent the wheel.

Good oils, if you choose to use them: Crown of Success, Boss Fix.

— catherineyronwode (M, AIRR)

• When will I start seeing results?

I have a honey jar with my lover's name and mine. For a whole week I used tea light candles on top of both jars in red and blue. However, I noticed that nothing happened. Therefore, I changed the tea light candles to the longer six inch candles and light them up every day and pray for what I want. I have been doing this for three days now.

My question is: How long for me to start seeing him looking for me?

— makemeright

One way to gauge results is by threes: three days to watch for a sign that the spell has started to work, three weeks to see movement or progress, and three months to wait for a final result. You may get the result you're looking for faster, but if you get no results within a three month time frame, you may consider that the spell has failed.

— Miss Bri (M, AIRR)

• Candy in a honey jar?

A guy who caught my eye didn't seem to notice me, or anything for that matter. So i got a small jar of honey, a red candle, one of his hairs, one of mine — and then an idea hit me right out of left field. Pixy Sticks.

Think about it, sticks of what's basically coloured sugar. What could be better for a honey jar? I had some laying around, mostly because I'm a little addicted to them, and I decided to use five red ones: three mixed into the honey and two poured on top.

It's definitely not "old school" but it worked well for me so i thought I'd share it. I figure at the very least someone may get a laugh out of it.

— Turnsteel

Hey, cool. I am not laughing. Your Pixy Sticks sugar idea is not all that different from an idea I have for a love potion I am making up for my mate and me.

I chose nine edible herbs and spices for love and passion to infuse in olive oil. I was thinking I would dissolve some Red Hots cinnamon candies in it. The saffron I have in it is making it a beautiful orange-red. I figure the Red Hots will be nice to punch up the flavour.

— EcleckticMama

• How do I burn candles on my honey jar?

I just completed a honey jar on a guy who I would like to be "sweeter" on me (i.e., more attentive). I did the hair, the herbs, the name-paper, etc., and spoke what I wanted. Then I dressed a four-inch red candle with Love Me Oil and am burning it. Should the candle burn all the way out or is there a time limit that I should snuff it out?

When I work the honey jar again on Wednesday, Friday, and Monday should I speak my desires again or meditate on it again?

— suzyparker

Let it burn out. That's the reason those candles are so small — each is one 'dose,' if you will. This is how I do it:

I dress each candle individually for use each time, and while I dress it, I pray extemporaneously to bless and charge the candle with my intention, etc. (For you this might be meditation, speaking of intentions or desires as applicable.) The key thing, though, is that after I'm done and have set the light atop the jar, I let all those wishes and desires go — and I just don't think about it the rest of the time.

— Silverpony

• Can I clean the wax from my honey jar?

I have had my honey jar for many months. Can I clean the wax melted on top? I'm going traveling and I want to take it with me.

— theusurper

Sure, you can. Some folks do, some don't. It's a matter of personal style.

— catherineyronwode (M, AIRR)

• Can white candles be burnt on a reconciliation honey jar?

Can I burn white candles on a reconciliation jar until I get pink ones?

— path2success

You can burn white candles for pretty much anything. Anoint them with the appropriate oils, just as you would with the pink candles.

— Miss Bri (M, AIRR)

• **After a vacation, do I need a new honey jar?**

I have been burning candles on my honey jar since the end of May, but I took a one-week vacation in the end of June. During my vacation, instead of burning candles, which I was not able to do, I prayed at night and visualized a candle burning in my head. I got back on my candle burning routine when I came back. The signs of candle burning have been good since day one, even though I have not seen any movements on my wishes. Does anyone think I should use a new honey jar or just keep using the old one? Any answer from experienced spell casters will be greatly appreciated.

— shuchingwu

Short answer: Keep using the old one! It's fine for a honey jar to sit a week, and added prayer always helps. "Visualization," on the other hand, is not traditional hoodoo. Ya gotta light the candle.

— deaconmillett (M, AIRR)

You don't give much info, so I don't know what you personally mean by "signs" and "movements."

I would like to address something that I see time and time again with honey jars and love work in general: Enjoying hopeful "signs," while suffering for a lack of work in the real world! I have been prone to this myself and let me tell you, it gets you *nowhere*. Burn the honey jar, but if you want to speak to him or her, then do so; listen to your instincts.

Put yourself in their presence, call them (do not stalk them), and see how your work is progressing. Is he or she "sweet" towards you? Is he or she open to a relationship with you?

There could be *tons* of movement you do not see!

My work was doing wonders on my current boyfriend and I did not even know it, because I was waiting for an email. I picked myself up and went to him and things went swimmingly. He was a bit scared of emailing me, because he was not sure about my feelings towards him. My gumption showed him my interest and he got his green light. We are very happy now.

Magic is an aid, but not the total answer. Your actions may have to carry some of the load.

— Literarylioness (M)

• How do I inscribe and anoint a candle?

I am new to hoodoo and was wondering, do you need to inscribe anything on the candle? Also, what is the best way to anoint oil onto a candle for the honey jar spell for increasing attraction.

— LMgroupie

It's always a good idea to at least inscribe the name of the person on the candle. A needle or a nail will work. Rub the oil in by hand to dress the candle. You do not need to be able to see the lettering once you have inscribed it and dressed it with oil.

— catherineyronwode (M, AIRR)

• Can I use a pretty jar sealed with a cork?

I found a jar I really like, but it's corked, not metal-capped. Can I use this? If I do use it, should I keep the jar refrigerated? (I'm not sure if that would "put the spell on ice," so to speak.)

—k_phoenix

I would not use a cork cap, because you will be burning candles on it. The cork could go up in flame or smoke. Small food jars with metal lids are the best for honey jars as they are compact and fireproof. Don't refrigerate the jar; you will only slow down or stop the work.

— Literarylioness (M)

• What is the best kind of candle to use?

What is the best type of candle that will burn safely on the honey jar?

— spellyshelly

I like the four inch offertory candles myself.

— Miss Bri (M, AIRR)

I also like birthday candles. You can dip them right into the oil.

— Literarylioness (M)

I start with a figural candle and then go to "chime" or "altar" candles.

— deaconmillett (M, AIRR)

• Can I get some pointers on my Lucky Mojo honey jar kit?

1. *Is it okay that i ordered a Love Me rather than a Reconciliation honey jar? I wasn't sure which one, as we've been friends since we split.*

2. The love herbs that came with the kit i only added to the petition-paper and did not sprinkle any in the actual honey. Is this okay?

3. My extra candles that i ordered with the kit don't sit well in the star shaped holder; they sit a bit lopsided.

4. I have noticed the candle holder is normally quite sooty.

5. A bit of the wax has now fallen down the side of honey jar like a stream — is this normal or a bad sign?"

— LMgroupie

1.Yes. Either one is fine.

2. That's fine, and it is the traditional way to work.

3. You are supposed to squeeze the prongs of the star candle holder inward until it very tightly fits whatever size candle you are using. You squeeze them in, then try a candle to see if it fits tight.

4. Yes, that's normal, after you've been burning candles in it.

5. A stream of wax like that indicates that tears will flow. See my web page on candle wax and candle glass divination here:

LuckyMojo.com/candlemagicdivination.html

— catherineyronwode (M, AIRR)

• What do I do if the honey is so thick that I can't shake it?

I've made two honey jars, one for my ex and one for his family, both containing normal clear honey. To my surprise the honey is set in both jars and it's very difficult to shake. Is this normal? Does this mean the work is stopped? I'm just on an override here.

— oceanblue

It's generally break-up and vinegar jars that are shaken, in order to make the needles and pins and glass and stuff poke and pierce the people who are targeted. Honey jars are treated gently. The honey getting thick shouldn't bother you — it happens naturally as the honey crystallizes. You can always warm the honey to loosen it up again, but it's not necessary.

— Devi Spring (M, AIRR)

• Can I put multiple people in one honey jar?

I'm getting ready to run a few jars.

First Jar: I'd like to put my friend's mother in a honey jar as well as friends to aid her in finding a job, using Crown of Success oil and powder. Would I have to petition a name-paper for each person or is there a way of adding everyone on one paper? Or could I write it as a petition letter, including their names once each? What format is recommended? What are platonic herbs and candle colours? Can I use pink and blue? Because I don't plan on seducing them romantically.

2nd Jar: I'd like to create one for my immediate family so we all live happily in peace and respect each other, and we all attract prosperity. Is there any way of adding everyone to the same jar? I plan on using Fiery Wall of Protection oil as well with this. I'm assuming pink and blue candles? I don't plan on seducing my brother.

3rd Jar: Is there one I can do for myself, to attract more platonic, helpful, genuine friends, prosperity, and popularity?

4th Jar: I'd like one for my friend, to attract the job she wants and an apartment as well. She's a good person, hit hard by bad luck.

— mimiso

For the 1st jar, you can put each person on an individual name-paper. Try to get a hair, a photo, or a business card. from each person. Use the business card as a name-paper. This allows you to add more names as you go along. Or you can use a Broom straw for each person, tie them to a piece of Master Root to represent the woman, and wrap it all in a petition-paper. Or you can write one petition folded around a series of small papers. Or you can write all the names on one paper. You do not want "platonic" herbs. You want success and business herbs. Complete lists can be found at the back of my book "Hoodoo Herb and Root Magic." I just gave you two — the Broom Straws and Master Root trick.

On the 2nd jar, Peaceful Home Oil on blue candles would be better than Fiery Wall of Protection Oil — it's a *honey* jar, not a protection spell. Use calming and happy home herbs like Basil, Rose, and Althaea.

For the other jars, use herbs and oils per HHRM, like Clove powder for friendship, Gravel Root for a job, and Five Finger Grass for an apartment.

— catherineyronwode (M, AIRR)

• Can I speed up the work?

Can someone recommend what I can add or feed a honey jar that can speed it up a bit or get it to work a little faster? Is that even possible?

—Isis

I was taught to burn an orange candle dressed with Road Opener Oil and deer's tongue leaves next to the honey jar. It helps open the way. As I dress the candle, I pray and focus on encouraging the guy to be more open in his communication and expressive with his feelings. It's worked quite well for me, even with guys who're rather introverted.

— cabriellenil

I'll use an accompanying vigil light to Saint Expedite, fixed with Fast Luck oil. He seems to like a bit of cinnamon sugar as well. Saint Expedite is the saint of speedy results. He is very clear. He will say yes or he'll say no — but at least you've given him the chance to come to your aid.

My friend ConjureMan Ali sometimes surrounds slow-acting honey jars with tea lights to warm the honey up and hasten their activity. My teacher, Miss Cat, uses four chime candles in star holders to surround the honey jar, lighting them East (dawn), South (noon), West (sunset), and North (midnight) to open the roads to the four directions. Try it!

— deaconmillett (M, AIRR)

• Can I use glass-encased candles on top of a honey jar?

I read that you're supposed to allow the wax from the candle to flow down over the honey jar. I've tried this, but when I try to light another candle on top of the previous wax left over, it is unstable and doesn't work. Can I use glass-encased candles on top of the honey jar instead or is the dripping wax essential to the spell?

— wasylena

I've never seen glass encased vigils used this way. Try the little brass candle holder stars that Lucky Mojo sells. Put one on top of the lid of the honey jar, set the candle in it, and let it burn. You still get wax drippings but you also have a stable base to put the candle on.

— Miss Bri (M, AIRR)

• **Did I mess up?**

I created my honey jar last night, but I want to know if I made a mistake. The only thing I placed in the name-paper, where I wrote our names and folded it, was his hair and mine. I just threw the herbs in the bottle. Was I supposed to wrap the herbs in the name-paper also? Also, I wrote my petition around our names without lifting the pen, but then I decided to write the petition below on the same paper and I did lift the pen. Is that a problem? If so I can do it again. I hope I didn't mess up.

—Simpleme

When I just started hoodoo I made a lot of little mistakes like that. Next time you could lay out all your ingredients and mentally rehearse the whole thing, even have a few 'reminders' written down if necessary. Try not to inject so much doubt in your work. Be confident.

— cabriellenil

Rehearsing your spells is actually a great habit. Not only does it help to make sure you don't miss anything, but it also engraves the spell really well into your mind. Rehearsing helps makes the spell organic, rather than a series of mechanical motions.

As for herbs, it is traditional to put them in the packet, not loose in the honey or sugar. Some prefer to place finely-cut herbs in the packet, while larger herb curios, such as cinnamon sticks, are placed whole in the honey or sugar. Candles may be dusted with powdered herbs.

Since you had a great deal of doubt, especially regarding the way you wrote the petition-paper, start over, but this time trust yourself.

— ConjureMan Ali (M, AIRR)

• **What if the name-paper sticks up out of the honey?**

Does it matter if a corner or part of the name-paper sticks up out of the honey a little? I don't want to open it to add more honey.

—Fairywinkle

Don't get too over-technical with it. Papers tend to float. As long as you can close the metal lid on the jar, you're fine.

—TBanks91

• **Do candle colours really matter?**

What are the best and most appropriate colours for love honey jars? Some spell books make mention that candle colours are important because they give a vibrational frequency that helps manifest your desired intentions. Although I've been using white candles, the idea of burning pink candles on the honey jar has been overwhelming, to the point that I've made the change and now feel relieved, although I still don't know why I experienced this.

— moondancer

You ask if the colours of the candles really have an effect — and then you tell us that you definitely noticed the difference when you changed from burning white candles to burning pink candles.

I think you just answered your own question.

— catherineyronwode (M, AIRR)

I do not feel that I answered my own question. I know there is always a cause and an effect to things and this is what I am trying to understand.

I know these things are tools and that the magic ultimately comes from you the petitioner, but when it comes to enhancing or strengthening a spell with herbs or oils, you have to know the why behind it. If it's just a dye that's been added to give it colour, is it really that important?

—moondancer

Coloured candles burn with a specific vibration, dictated in large part by the colour of the wax. So if you are able to use that extra bit of tuning — great! If you cannot (for instance, if you were born colour-blind), then you will not detract from your work by using a plain white candle.

But I can tell you that if you go to do your spell and your head is all spinning with the 'whys' and 'hows' and questions about minute details of the mechanics and physics of everything, you're going to have a tough time concentrating on the spiritual and magical work at hand.

You want to turn everything over to your intuition at that point — the very intuition you don't seem to want to trust as your teacher.

— Devi Spring (M, AIRR)

In discussing the best colours for a love honey jar, moondancer wrote, "the magic ultimately comes from you the petitioner."

This belief is not the basis of hoodoo. It is, however, the basis of Neo-Pagan magic and New Age affirmation magic.

In hoodoo we work with spirits and with God. The spirits include those of angels, ancestors, the dead, animals, and herbs; even minerals are considered to be alive and spiritually aware. Thus "the magic" — our successful jobs — are the result of working with spiritual allies.

We may additionally add visual reinforcement to our work in the form of special colours for our candles, cloth bags, or altar coverings, in order to help us focus our intentions better and to attract like-minded spirits — but in the end, it is the *spirits* and our *prayers*, not a candle colour and not our mere selves — that accomplish the work.

In sweetening spells, we are either working with the honey that Bees have extracted and refined from sweet nectar-rich flowers or with the sweet refined essences of plants. These sweet flowering plants (and the Bees) are our spiritual allies. Because many flowers that smell sweet and attract Bees are pink and red, and because the menstrual blood or oestral blood of mammals is red, and because babies are born with blood, we look to colours like pink for romance and red for the passion that leads to sex and birth.

But here's the thing: In hoodoo, it is not only about *us* — it is about *spirit* and *prayer*, so a pink candle is more significant if we carve it with our lover's name and smear it with an oil made with sweet flower essences and with our menstrual blood, and place it on top of a honey jar in which we have captured the physical tokens of our lover — hair, fingernails, a photo, a name and birthdate.

Then we pray — we call on God, and on our ancestors who had happy marriages to come to our aid, we call on the sweetness of the honey and the way that the Bees made it from nectar to refine the sweetness in our lovers' heart, we ask the spirits of the beautiful sweet Roses and Honeysuckles and the reckless sexual abandon of the Juniper berries, and the spicy heat of Ginger to infuse and enflame the mind and body of the one we love.

It is the whole company of spirits and allies, not just "the practitioner" that accomplishes this work.

— catherineyronwode (M, AIRR)

• Can I use one jar for friendship and love? Can I use a photo?

Does the shape of the candle you put on the honey jar really matter? Is it possible to alternate a jar between being used for friendship and romance? Would putting their photo in or under the jar help?

— neverfit

The shape of a candle may be an excellent aid to your visual and spiritual focus, but beyond that it is does not "matter." Some rootworkers use figural candles, while others use chime candles, birthday candles, or even tea lights. All are equally effective. If you are working on a particular person, you can indeed alternate the candles, white and pink for friendship and romance and red for love and passion.

Photos are used either in the jar or under it, but usually not in both places. If you have photos of each of you, dab honey on the lips in each photo and pray as you hold them face to face, as if the pictures of you two were kissing. Then you can fold in your herbs as you fold your petition towards you. Put your packet in the honey, so that the honey will sweeten the relationship.

— ConjureMan Ali (M, AIRR)

• What if I don't have time to burn a candle?

Even if I burn the candle for maybe 5 or 10 minutes on some nights, would this be effective, or should the candle burn down all at once? Also, if I haven't worked my honey jar for a while, will it "re-activate" once I burn the candle and pray over it? Or should I make a new one?

—Angelina

The idea is that you are letting the fire of your intention or desire heat up the spell contained within the honey by having the candle burn all the way down. You can purchase four-inch candles from Lucky Mojo which last about 1.5 hours, or use a tea light or birthday candle. All of these options will accommodate your timing and still get the conjure going. If you still can't do it, then I suggest letting the candle burn for at least 15 minutes, twice a day. I've seen people work that time frame and it was fine for them. Just pinch out the candle when you are done.

— ConjureMan Ali (M, AIRR)

• What kind of prayers should I use?

I have a honey jar spell. What kinds of prayers and to whom should I say over the candle as I anoint and light it?

— kmew1315

If this is your first time doing a reconciliation honey jar spell I suggest you start with Psalms 51 and a white candle. Hyssop works wonders and white is the colour of a new start between you and your ex.

— Dr Johannes (M, AIRR)

Psalms 45 and 46 are also used for reconciliation. Psalms 23 is wonderful, and Psalms 138 is great if you are drawing a new love to your life. I use the Song of Solomon when it comes to love work. The complete Book of Psalms, with magical uses, is online here:

ReadersAndRootworkers.org/wiki/Category:The_Book_of_Psalms

— Papa Newt (M)

• Is a bigger jar better? How long will it take?

I have heard that a sweet spell takes longer to manifest than other spells, but once it starts working, it has a powerful effect. Is this correct?

The Lucky Mojo mini honey kit I bought comes in a jar just a little bigger than the size of baby food jar, and i was wondering if it needs to be larger — that is, will it be just as strong as a bigger jar?

— lmlvr

Honey jars can have a powerful affect. I like to think of them as the endurance runners of hoodoo. They work gradually but when done correctly I have seen them work very consistently as well.

The size of your jar is not as important as you may think. The idea is to cover the petition, doll, or other items in sweetness, and since most petitions and bottle-spell dolls are small, there is no need for a large jar.

However, if you are working on a bunch of people, and if you intend to use the sugar or honey from your spell-work in cooking for them, as part of a long-term sneaky trick, then you may want to have an extra amount for that purpose, and it would be a good idea to start with a larger jar.

— Miss Bri (M, AIRR)

• Are more herbs, more oils, and bigger petitions better?

In addition to personal effects, do more herbs, powders, and oils intensify the powers of the honey jar? Is a photocopy of his signature a good item to add to a honey jar as well as other personal effects?

Can you write more then one command on your petition, say using two circles, one on the outside and a smaller one inside it? I want to ensure complete love and fidelity as we live in different states. I don't know if one circle will be big enough to write both commands.

— arieschic72

More is not better. You don't really need more than a pinch of botanicals, not counting large items like whole roots or lodestones, and too much oil on a candle is actually a bad idea. That's why the dram vial of oil with Lucky Mojo honey jar kits lasts so long. If you have better personal concerns, skip his signature. You mention "commands," but please remember that honey jars are for sweetening, not for ruling or controlling people. I wouldn't make two circles on the petition, just one. A good way to do it would be to say something like "Honesty Love Fidelity" And just repeat the words going around in a circle. Or write a letter as a petition.

— Turnsteel

• What kind of pen should I use?

1. The pen used to write the petition: If it's not water proof, is it a problem, as i think the names might get erased when immersed in honey.

2. When i burn the candles, no wax remains except a few tears.

—Basilthyme

Pencilled writing is relatively resistant to water, making this one reason to consider using a pencil in writing out a petition-paper. However, in practical application, water-soluble pen-ink shouldn't present a problem on a folded petition-paper immersed in honey. Indeed, if your petition text is dissolved into the honey, the essence of the prayer may be even more intensely present in the work.

Wax tears during the burn may indicate emotional fallout, but if the candles are burning cleanly, that is a good sign.

— Lukianos (M, AIRR)

• **Will two honey jars make the spell stronger?**

Can I make two sugar jars using the same person's name in each to make the spell stronger?

— sweet-12

No, that is a total waste of your time and energy. A spell jar is a *tool.* If you want to hammer a nail, you get one good hammer and learn how to use it. Trying to hammer a nail with two hammers will not make the work go faster, better, or stronger.

— catherineyronwode (M, AIRR)

• **How do you get candles to stay on the jar?**

How do you get thin candles to stay upright on the jar?

— daviscol

Thin candles can be mounted on a jar lid by lightly flaming the bottom of the candle to melt the wax a little and then pressing the softened end of the candle onto the jar lid. The wax should re-harden relatively quickly, and the candle will then be stuck in place.

— Lukianos (M, AIRR)

• **What is the best day of the week to start a honey jar?**

What is the best day of the week, if any, to start a honey jar?

— csrs

Depends on what the jar is for. And then it's really up to you whether you take timing into consideration; not all workers do.

— Devi Spring (M, AIRR)

Most people work their honey jars every day or every Monday, Wednesday, and Friday. For details on using other days of the week, see LuckyMojo.com/planetary.html.

— starsinthesky7 (M)

Today is the best day to start your honey jar.

— deaconmillett (M, AIRR)

• Can I restart an old honey jar?

I made a love honey jar for my ex, used it, and it worked. However, long story short, I need to do another one. I never disposed of the original, so I have been using fresh candles and burning them on this old honey jar. Do you think it will work?

— lizabeth

I have personally had success restarting an old one for the *same* guy.

— suzyparker

• How do I choose a time for the work?

I've been studying white magick for about two months now and it emphasizes the importance of timing. Is rootwork the same way or no?

— moondancer

Sugar and honey spells that include candles seem to work best if you set a regular schedule for burning the lights. One traditional timing is Monday for healing, Wednesday for communication, Friday for love. Another is to burn the candle for 15 minutes every morning and evening. Some of us work by the Moon's waxing and waning phases, some by the Moon's course through the Zodiacal signs, and some work only "by need."

Another form of timing concerns the duration of the spell work itself. Some folks work a spell "for as long as it takes" — and then find that it never completes. I suggest that you start by setting yourself clear goals and establish a time-frame in which to work, steadily praying both your goals and your time-frame into the spell. For instance, each day, after making a prayer and lighting a candle for reconciliation, you may close with a vow such as, "I will work this spell for three months, until June 1st, and during these three months i will attempt to contact [Name] three times, each time with sincerity, humility, and gentle love in my heart, and i will accept the results God gives me, Amen."

Watch for signs, look for movement, and abide by your vow.

— catherineyronwode (M, AIRR)

For more on spell timing, see "Astrology for Rootworkers" in **"The Black Folder" edited by Catherine Yronwode**

• What days should I work my honey jar?

I'm working on a honey jar now, a friendship one. I've read that you should do Monday, Wednesday, and Friday for honey jar work, but Fridays are best for relationship work. I've also read that when starting out, you should do it for 3 days then once a week, but I've also read you should do it for multiples of 7 days (7, 14, 21, etc.), then once a week. What way is best?

—remyq

Honey and sugar jars are worked a number of ways with respect to how many candles are burned and how often. All are effective, none is better than another. They're just different, worker to worker. A few examples:

1. Burn candles on a love jar Monday-Wednesday-Friday, either all red, all pink or all blue; or burn blue on Monday, pink on Wednesday, and red on Friday.
2. Burn candles on an employment jar Tuesday-Wednesday-Thursday, either all purple, all green, or all yellow; or burn purple on Tuesday, yellow on Wednesday, and green on Thursday.
3. Burn a candle once a week on an established honey or sugar jar so as to "refresh" it and keep the good stuff going.
4. Burn a candle daily to get things moving more quickly.
5. Burn a candle three times daily on a honey jar, surround it with candles, or heat it lightly in simmering water, to put heat on a situation.

If you still feel uncertain, you can hire a magical coach to guide you.

—aura (M)

• Do I eat the honey every day I work my honey jar?

Am I supposed to take a spoonful of honey and eat it each and every time before I burn the candle on top?

— JustinSane23

The taste of the honey accompanies the "as this is sweet ..." statement when you assemble the honey jar. You need not taste of it each time you work the jar, though the honey can be used to sweeten the target of the spell's food and drink, and you can eat it then as well.

— Doctor Hob (M)

• **How long do honey jars normally take to work?**

How long do honey jars normally take to work? I have read that honey jars take so long to manifest.

— Tash

I am not sure what you mean when you say,"I have read that honey jars take so long to manifest." *How* long have you heard that they take? Because i know they can work very quickly or at a slower pace, but that what is really most important is to not consider *no action* as a sign that action will manifest *later*. I mean, *no action* is just that — *no action.*

Nine days should be enough to at least get you going the way you want on a sugar bowl or honey jar.

Why do i say that? Because nine days is the minimum number of days that my old teachers recommended for a complete honey jar Court Case spell: "no less than nine days." (They can be worked for longer, of course.) So if you think or were told that sweet spells take six months or more to work — well, that's just not true, in my experience.

— catherineyronwode (M, AIRR)

• **Can I cut the hair? What if it doesn't have the root?**

Is it okay to cut down a long strand of hair to use in a jar spell or should one just go with the whole strand? I was thinking to conserve the hair because I've only got a few long strands, but I don't want to weaken the item by alteration of it, so what is the correct way to do this?

— loveliesbleeding

You can cut the hair.

— catherineyronwode (M, AIRR)

I understand that to make the honey jar be more successful your hair and the other person's hair is very important. I do not have the root of the hair. I was cutting his hair and collected that. Is the root needed or not?

— supper

No, the root of the hair is not needed. This isn't a nuclear DNA test!

— deaconmillett (M, AIRR)

• **Do I have to use personal concerns from both of us?**

If this was intended for only sweetening the man, would combining his semen and my menstrual blood be okay? Will it sweeten both of us as a couple? Or will it make me act even sweeter when I am already sweet to this man? I want us to be equal or have him be sweeter than me.

— lmlvr

When working with personal concerns, you have a choice.

If you are using the item as a token to identify the party whom you wish to sweeten, then you need not add your own personal concerns.

If the honey or sugar jar spell is intended to mate the two of you, however, then i recommend that you "match" two items, one from each of you, because placing them in contact within the sweetener is a symbol of placing the two of you in contact in a world of sweetness.

When matching items, it is nice if they are of a similar quality, so it is the custom to match together two hairs, two samples of bodily fluids, two handwriting samples, and so forth, to make neat pairs.

— catherineyronwode (M, AIRR)

• **My lover is bald...what do I do?**

My lover is bald ... what do I do for my honey jar?

—jwmcclin (M)

Does he shave or trim a beard? Clean out the razor, or pick up facial hairs from the counter and around the sink.

Pick up pubic hairs from the toilet bowl rim under the seat. I use baby wipes every time I use it, so I know they are his hairs.

Clean out your hair from the sink, shower, or tub drains each time you use them and check for his hairs after he uses the facilities.

Check all around the bathroom. Hair accumulates everywhere. Does he have chest and leg hair that falls on the bathroom floor?

Study and compare and you will be able to tell that it's his hair, especially if you are fastidious about keeping things clean of your hair.

Hair, it's there, somewhere.

I have no shame when I am determined to get biological concerns.

— venusofwillendorf

• How do I write without lifting my hand?

I have just received my Lucky Mojo honey jar and I am very excited, however, I am still confused about how to properly write the petition around in a circle without lifting my hand, dotting i's, and crossing t's.

— concernedmom

It's like cursive writing, only join *all* the letters — no break between words. Once the circle is complete, go back to dot the i's and cross the t's.

— Devi Spring (M, AIRR)

• Should I use a picture of both of us together?

I have no picture of him alone, only a picture we took of each other together during a happy time. I figure we need to be nicer to each other.

— Mechii

If it's a honey jar for love, then the picture of both of you together can work well. If both partners contributed mutually to the difficulties (often the case), it can help a lot to address both of you in the jar.

There are a lot of variations on sweetening spells, so just like in jazz, if you understand the principles, there is some space for improvisation.

— aura (M)

• How do I add sexual fluids — and whose?

How do you go about adding sexual fluids (from both parties) to a honey jar? And is it okay to add combined sexual fluids to honey jars, because it seems this is not a good thing to do with nation sacks.

— jazzie

Dabbing the fluids on a string or cloth and placing it in your petition-paper packet works well. You don't want to mix your and your man's fluids in a nation sack because a nation sack is a form of female domination and you don't want to mix yourself into that kind of a spell. For a honey jar meant to keep you sweet together I think that if the fluids are mixed you're okay, because a bit of sweetening never hurt no one.

— Turnsteel

• How long do my prayers have to be?

If pushed for time, what is the quickest format of prayer that could be done that would still be effective? Could I light a candle on the jar, say a short prayer to the saint I'm working with, and run? Do you go through the whole of your petition that is in your jar and what's under the jar, every time you do jar work? Even if your jar has been ongoing for six months?

— magictinkerbell

Prayer in hoodoo is similar to prayer in most Protestant traditions (because hoodoo is mostly an African-American Protestant magical tradition) and is pretty solidly based in the Psalms. I find that, after reading the same Psalm every day for a week, I have it about half-memorized.

So, yes, there is certainly room for a quick prayer-n-go, but you must take enough time to fix your attention on the work!

— MissMichæle (M, AIRR)

If i have worked a sugar jar for a while and realize i won't have time to attend to it because i must do something else, i place my hand on it, close my eyes, and say, "Keep on working 'til i come back again, in the name of Jesus Christ, amen." (I never noticed before, but that rhymes, kinda.)

— catherineyronwode (M, AIRR)

• I put my name under my target's name. Now what?

I just started my honey jar and wrote my name first three times than his name three times over my name. Everything else I did correctly. I can't believe I did this. What should I do?

— jwmcclin (M)

Well, you could take the paper out and remake it right and put it in the jar, or you could leave it as is. You may have given him the edge in the relationship, but it's a spell for sweetness, not domination, so it won't hurt anyone. We all make mistakes, and we all move on and try to take our lessons from what we've done. Here the lesson would probably be to work from a state of mindfulness and make sure you've done things in a way that you're happy with and that are appropriate to your goals.

— Turnsteel

• Can I put condition oils in my honey jar?

Is it okay to add a drop of some Lucky Mojo oils in my honey jar?
— Angelina

Oils are generally used to dress candles that are set on sweet jars. People may wish to eat the sugar or honey, or to cook with it and serve the food to the target. The dressing oils are not guaranteed to be edible.
— Lukianos (M, AIRR)

• Magnets in a honey jar?

Years ago I had someone perform a honey jar spell for me. It worked great — within a week. It was a reconciliation spell. The only unusual thing was that once all of the items were folded within the paper, the paper was then placed between two magnets, which were then tied with a red ribbon and put in the jar. Has anyone else ever heard of doing this? He also had me burn a candle for seven straight days at the same time every evening, while meditating on my desired outcome, but he told me not to burn it on top of the jar, but next to it. I had to bury the jar in a pot or in my backyard. I wanted to repeat the spell, as obviously it had worked before, so I was going to try a similar method. Any thoughts?
— kansas

The magnets make for a nice variation on a lodestone spell — a little less chunky, a little more "modern." Not all sugar or honey spells have a candle on top — or even have a candle at all. Backyard burial keeps 'em close to home, and is quite traditional. Sounds like a nice spell.
— deaconmillett (M, AIRR)

• How many cloves do I put in a honey jar?

How many cloves would you use if you are putting more than one person in the honey jar?
— spellyshelly

One for each person, including yourself or not, as you see fit.
— Literarylioness (M)

• How do I sweeten my mom to my boyfriend?

I'm trying a honey jar to sweeten my mom to my boyfriend. I don't want to put in things that are associated with romantic love. I'm looking for herbs that have to do with unconditional love and empathy. Any suggestions?

— battleship

Basil, rosemary, and periwinkle are always a good start when trying to make family members get along — and that's the eventual goal, right? Motherwort may get her to imagine him as a "son." Lavender and cloves are good at establishing friendship and harmony. Balm of Gilead buds will help if they fight. And hyssop will help them forgive and forget.

— Deacon Millett (M, AIRR)

• Must I create a new jar to make additions?

I have been told that it's better to create a new honey jar than to open a jar and make additions. I need only to add deer's tongue, so can I just add the herb in the honey, because creating another jar would mean burning candles on both of them or disposing of the first one, but it is done perfectly so I don't want to dispose of it.

What is the normal burn time of a four-inch Lucky Mojo candle — just to ensure my candle is not burning too fast or too slow.

— path2success

"Better to create a new honey jar than to open a jar and make additions?" Not that i know of, and i've been doing this for 50 years. Some spells do require closure, but people open and add things to sugar bowls and honey jars all the time. We take sugar out and cook with it and top it up again. Just be sure that any herbs you add are *edible*, as tasting the honey or sugar when you add things is a vital part of the spell.

I was taught to include herbs in a paper packet, not loose in the honey, like sloppy stew. Make a new packet for the Deer's Tongue from a second name-paper. That way the honey remains clean enough to cook with. Ditto for sugar. You don't want loose herbs in your sugar bowl, do you?

Our four-inch altar candles last about an hour to an hour and a half.

— catherineyronwode (M, AIRR)

• Can I use cayenne pepper to "heat things up"?

I used cayenne pepper with the intention of "bringing hot passionate sex." I've now read that cayenne brings anger, which explained why we had a huge blow up last Friday. Should I redo my honey jar?

— GoldenFlow7

Remake the jar and add cinnamon for hot spicy results.

— jwmcclin (M)

Add ginger instead. Hot and spicy, but also sweet. Good for hot sex.

— Turnsteel

Ginger and Cinnamon are "happy hot spices" as opposed to Cayenne Pepper, which is an "angry hot spice" that can burn like the dickens if you don't use it right! Cinnamon is also used for wealth and Ginger is also used for protection. Cardamom is another love-spice. The pods look neat in a sugar jar, and are large enough to sift out when you cook with the sugar.

— catherineyronwode (M, AIRR)

• Do I need to hide my honey jar?

My altar is in sight of everyone, so do I need to hide the jar?

— msangela

If all the people you live with are 100% supportive of your work and have absolutely no negative thoughts about it, then it should be fine. You shouldn't discuss ongoing work, so if people are going to be talking about it, then you may very well want to consider hiding it.

— Devi Spring (M, AIRR)

• Should I roll my candle in sachet powder?

I was going to roll my candle in sachet powder. Is that okay?

—remyq

Rolling oiled candles in powders is a very old-fashioned "woman's way" of working, very traditional, and highly favoured by many.

— catherineyronwode (M, AIRR)

• How do I count the number of ingredients?

I've been told that you're supposed to use an odd number of ingredients in a honey jar. Does the honey count as an ingredient?

— Fairywinkle

Do keep in mind that ingredient-counting is done differently by different people, depending on how they were taught, and that many conjure doctors were never taught a system of counting or, perhaps, decided to ignore counting and to just put in what's necessary to do the job. I've never counted honey or sugar as an ingredient.

—aura (M)

• Can I use Essence of Bend-Over or I Dominate My Man Oil?

Can I use Essence of Bend-Over Oil on the candle that I burn on top of the honey jar? Would it help to sweeten and command the one I love at the same time? How about I Dominate My Man Oil?

— FeelingaPerfect7

Essence of Bend-Over Oil with a honey jar? Why would you want to do that? It doesn't even make sense to me. Like beating a puppy and then expecting it to be sweet to you. I wouldn't. There are much gentler oils that you can use to get the upper hand without commanding.

I think I Dominate My Man Oil is too coercive to use with a honey jar, too. Not to say you can't use it, but I wouldn't use it with a honey jar. If you need to use it, use it with other spells.

Remember, the honey jar is to sweeten him. It's gentle! How do you act when you're with someone you want to sweeten? You're not in their face telling them to do what you say. You're gentle, sweet, flattering. As we like to say in the South, "Butter wouldn't melt in your mouth."

You can change him — but a honey jar isn't forceful. I see it as a way of leading him around to your point of view — by letting him think he's in charge. You're using a carrot, not a stick, to bring him around. That sort of thing takes time.

The more coercive, dominating oils and powders belong with other spells, in my humble opinion.

— d1angel

• What oils would be good for a lesbian relationship?

I wanted some advice on what oils would be good to mix with my Reconciliation Oil for the candle on my jar. This is for a lesbian relationship, and I have asked Lucky Mojo to burn a Lavender Love candle, to help get the ball rolling.

I don't know what else would be good for my situation. I broke up with my ex in August and since then it's been an emotional roller coaster of highs and lows, intimacy and arguments. We are currently not talking but that could change as soon as it started and we could be in each others arms by the weekend, just due to the nature of our relationship.

It is very confusing and hurtful and I want things to go back to how they were before we broke up.

—Tash

Reconciliation Oil is good by itself, but if, in addition to having arguments, you are also physically separated, you can add Return To Me Oil to increase proximity.

There are LGBT-oriented love oils which can be added to any of the general-purpose love oils — Lavender Love Drops and Q [Queer] Oil are quite well known in this regard. Another oil regularly purchased by my lesbian customers is Queen Elizabeth Root in Oil, and among very butch women, John the Conquer Oil has found favour.

Any of these oils, singly or blended, will be good to dress a candle burned on top of or next to a sugar bowl or honey jar. You may also wish to use Peace Water as a room spray to keep tempers calm.

— catherineyronwode (M, AIRR)

• Is licorice root in a honey jar a good idea?

Has anyone tried licorice root in a honey jar? Could it be a good idea?

—K54

Licorice root is used if you want the upper hand in a relationship and to have dominating power. When I work honey jars, I usually want sweetness, so I select something that is more gentle in nature, although I suppose that in certain situations licorice root can be a good additive.

— Miss Bri (M, AIRR)

• Can I use a sigil or seal? What herbs keep a lover faithful?

My honey jar is to keep my lover faithful. I was thinking of cinnamon sticks, cloves, and rose petals, wrapped up in real parchment with the petition in a circle with a sigil of Venus. What do you think?

—bubba

The cloves are good for friendship, and rose for love. Both the *Greater Key of Solomon* as well as the *6th and 7th Books of Moses* contain seals of Venus. On the back of the seal, write his name three times in black and cross it with yours three times in red, with the petition around it.

— J Simulcik

Since you are very concerned with fidelity, I would also suggest vanilla bean, coriander seeds, cumin seeds, lavender flower buds, rosemary, saffron, and cardamom, since they are all powerful love herbs. But remember, sweetening spells are for sweetness, not to force (or enforce) fidelity in one who is untrue. You may need a nation sack.

— EcleckticMama

• Will genital-shaped candles help us get physical?

I've been doing this honey jar on someone I'm sweet on at work. At first the candle would burn completely down which I know means it's working. The last two burns there was some wax. To be honest the wax seemed to form two hearts facing each other; it was kind of weird.

I like the sweetening effect. but we still haven't been physical. I was thinking of ordering the "private parts" candles from Lucky Mojo and giving them a try. Will that "heat" things up between us physically?

— sunseer88

The two hearts facing each others sounds like a great sign to me.

You might want to think about anointing the candle with your sexual fluids if you want the person to think of you sexually. With genital candles, anoint them with your own fluids in a very X-Rated kind of way, if you catch my meaning. I have been told that it is very effective.

— Turnsteel

• What is the safest way to burn a candle?

It's really hard to burn a candle in secret, since one needs to watch the candle so the house doesn't burn down. Do I have to stand over the candle until it burns out, or can I just say my wishes as I am lighting it?

— RosaMona

The most safe place is the bathtub. Do it early, before the sun rises.

— theusurper

In the oven or fireplace has been suggested as a good place too.

— Chagrinedgirl

For extra safety put the jar with the candle in a dish of sand, salt, or dirt. You can also try putting foil under it. Not only will this help with fireproofing and protecting whatever surface (counter, table, altar, etc.) you are burning candles on, but it will add intensity to your spell.

— Mama Micki (M)

Neither sugar spells nor honey spells *require* candles. If you can't burn candles safely, just prepare a different form of sugar or honey spell.

— catherineyronwode (M, AIRR)

• How much oil to use? Is it edible?

How much anointing oil do I put in the honey? Is it edible?

— spellyshelly

You don't want to stir loose conjure oils into a jar of honey or sugar, because tasting the sweetener is part of the rite of preparation and some essential oils are derived from toxic plants. You cannot safely taste anything that has had those oils stirred in.

The same goes for stirring loose toxic herbs into a sugar bowl or honey jar; that is not a good idea either.

You can dab a few drops of oil on the petition-paper (for instance, in a five-spot pattern) and you will dress the candle with oil, of course. You can combine several oils as well, according to your situation.

— Miss Bri (M, AIRR)

• **Are ants a bad sign?**

I noticed ants crawling on my honey jar. Is that a bad sign?
— nemesis

I would kill those ants and prevent that from happening. I wouldn't want something that could have an effect on the jar.
— msg33

I found out that ants got into my jar and so i panicked. I poured away the honey into the sink. Now i am wondering: Did i screw myself big time because i poured the first contents away in the sink?
— blackforrest

First, please do not use poison sprays on yourself or the environment. If you have Ants on your honey jar, there are only two reasons — the outside of the jar is not clean and / or it is not sealed tight. So clean it off — wash it with soapy water — and make sure it is tightly sealed.

Second, Ants are not a "bad sign." Quite the contrary! Ants occupy a special place in African-American hoodoo. They are thought to be great communicators, and it is said — and zoologically it may be true — that they are in contact with other Ants all over the world. Each nest of Ants defends its territory at the boundaries, and communicates through scent with the next Ants' nest over, and at their far end, they communicate with the next nest of Ants. So, just like human nations, they have relationships with and among one another. For this reason, there are many old-time hoodoo spells in which we call upon Ants to deliver a message of love — or anger — to someone far away. In fact, a great way to finish a honey or sugar spell is to open the jar at an Ant hill so that the Ants may carry it on.

Now, we don't want Ants tracking through our homes these days — and those of us who do not live rural, country lives are intolerant of them — but all we need to do to avoid contact with them is keep our glass jars clean and they will look elsewhere for food.

If they do come around, consider them messengers and ask them to carry your petition to the next nest of Ants over, and then to the next nest — kinda like a relay race or the Pony Express mail delivery system — and have them working for you.

— catherineyronwode (M, AIRR)

• Why did the target of my work get so mad at me?

I am a novice to all of this and totally confused. I started a honey jar on Friday. I accidentally ran into the target on Monday. The meeting was disastrous. He was angry and rude, and I don't like drama so I walked away. Each candle I have burned from that time on leaves a bunch of wax on the jar. Am I doing something wrong?

— mamigrl

Honey jars may take a bit of time to work, and sometimes people are rude and cold before the ice breaks and they become sweet and loving. But also be aware that unburned wax can be divined as unfinished business from the past: There may be a lot of negativity in this person's past that your honey jar is unable to move. You are doing nothing wrong.

— ConjureMan Ali (M, AIRR)

• Will a sweetening spell stop my boyfriend trying to control me?

I'm working on my boyfriend to sweeten him because lately he has been very controlling with me, constantly checking my phone, banning me from talking to people from my old job, imposing curfews. He is married and I was also married when we started but I am divorced and it's been seven years I've been with him and I've never been with anyone else.

— Sofia

Sugar may sweeten him, but there are other issues involved. You might also try a white skull candle dressed with Healing Oil while working towards assuaging his fears and helping him overcome his insecurity, but be aware that by imposing bans and curfews on you, he may have crossed a line which simple sweetening cannot ameliorate.

— ConjureMan Ali (M, AIRR)

Your boyfriend's distrust is not unwarranted, since you have both shown your willingness to cheat on your spouses. How he chooses to act on this distrust is another matter. Banning, curfews, and controlling are not signs of love from a partner. They may in fact be the start of a long and slippery slope of abuse. Be careful.

— deaconmillett (M, AIRR)

• **What should I do about a mouldy honey jar?**

I was turning my honey jar tonight when I discovered mould growing at the bottom. I think it's just remnants of the spaghetti sauce that was originally in the jar (very hard to clean out completely).

I don't want to ruin or negate the progress made with the old jar and the commands inside by just dumping it out, but I also don't want to think of the fact that mould is growing in my "inactive" jar.

If I'm wrong about the spaghetti sauce, do you think the mould is indicative of anything? Is it normal for mould to grow?

— nubiandiva

Mould does not normally grow in honey. If syrup is made with water, mould will grow in the syrup. It's usually greenish and floats on top. Don't mistake crystallizing honey for "mouldy" honey. Natural honey almost always crystallizes over time, with a white crystalline structure "growing" in the honey, often from the bottom. These are sugar crystals. Sugar crystals are normal. Mould means you have a problem.

— starsinthesky7 (M)

Everything in a conjure job has a relevant context, and so does your mould. Cleanse and make a new one. Sometimes a cigar is just cigar. But never in a hoodoo spell.

— Dr Johannes (M, AIRR)

As a reader, i'd say you didn't think this thing through. First, this is a honey jar, for sweetening; it is not a coercive jar to fill with "commands." Second, a person who does not know how to wash and sterilize a jar to put clean honey into needs to learn some basic kitchen skills before undertaking spell-casting. Honey is a preservative and will never grow mould on its own. So either your honey simply crystallized and you are ignorant about honey, or you worked dirty and got dirty results. If it truly is mouldy spaghetti sauce, dump it out. Then use hot water and soap to clean your glass jar. Clean the inside of the lid too. Pay attention to details. Like Dr. Johannes said, the untidy result you got was not an accident, but rather the effect of your own carelessness, and that carelessness is manifested in the spell now. Undo the damage and start anew.

— catherineyronwode (M, AIRR)

• My honey jar caught on fire. Do I need protection now?

I am in a daze right now. This morning my honey jar caught on fire. I have been lighting it since August, and have never had this happen. Fire was spewing from the canister where I keep the honey jar, I tried to put it out and the flames ignited and caught some of my hair on fire in the front. I was in total shock. Also this morning, my son became mysteriously ill. He has been vomiting all morning. I feel I need some protection. Do I continue the honey jar, risking further turmoil?

— Angel09

First off take a deep breath. Sometimes when we are working with fire, things go wrong. It does not always mean there is something magical going on. As a precaution, you can start by spiritually cleansing the house and your family with 13-Herb Bath, Uncrossing Bath and Chinese Wash.

As for your son, take him to the doctor, forget any magical attacks at this time, and deal with the illness with a professional medical doctor.

Regarding the honey jar: My gut tells me it is time to either clean up or stop this honey jar. Going forward you should consider fire safety and avoid building up wax and partially-burned wicks "in a canister."

— Leah Rivera (M)

When wax, oils, wicks, and herbs are allowed to build up on any altar space — a sugar box, a honey jar, or a simple candle stand — the danger of fire increases. It is your responsibility as a practicing spiritual worker to learn common-sense fire safety, just as you would in your kitchen.

From what you describe, you placed a honey jar inside a metal canister and never cleaned it out, creating a serious fire hazard. From a practical point of view, this accounts for what happened, without needing to look to an enemy attack or a counter-spell as a source from which you might need protection. This is not about the sweet spell. It is about fire safety.

Your hair catching on fire was dangerous! Had you been wearing flammable clothing, you could have been seriously burned! Everyone who works with candle flame on the altar, whether for sweetening or for any other purpose, should have proper candle tools, including a small fire extinguisher. There is a list of necessary candle tools in my book "The Art of Hoodoo Candle Magic" and i suggest that you check it out.

— catherineyronwode (M, AIRR)

• Can I put herbs and tea lights on top of a honey jar?

One time, my previous jar caught on fire onto my tablecloth when I fell asleep for a moment. I added too many herbs on the lid of the jar so that's what happened. Now I'm using tea lights with no metal containers and placing them on top, anointed with oil. Is that okay or not?

— lmlvr

When things catch on fire on your altar, it can be a sign about the work — and it can also be the result of carelessness with flammable materials. I have never put herbs on top of my honey jars — normally the herbs would be inside the name-packet in the jar, and the candle would be dressed with a conjure oil of the appropriate sort. So, please, don't put flammable herbs next to a burning candle. The same is true for burning tea lights without their metal containers. The wax in tea lights has a low melting point and is designed to melt in the metal container, for safety reasons. You might also try using birthday candles or some other small vertical (upright) candle, such as Hanukkah or Sabbath candles, that are designed to self-consume utterly and will not melt all over and make a fire-hazardous mess.

— catherineyronwode (M, AIRR)

• My honey jar blew its top. Twice!

Twice now I've had my honey jar swell up while burning a candle, as if it built up pressure and released it. Is my target "blowing his top"?

— rosepetals

A glass jar with a screw-down metal lid should not "swell up" unless you merely mean that the metal lid "popped" due to changes in temperature.

— deaconmillett (M, AIRR)

• What do I do if I get a hole in my honey jar?

If you get a hole in a honey jar should you start over?

— IBMagnet

A hole? In a glass jar with a metal lid? If you burned so many candles that you burned through a metal lid, get a new lid for your honey jar.

— ConjureMan Ali (M, AIRR)

• Should I worry if the residual wax melted off my honey jar?

I had a small puddle of wax that was left on the top of the lid from previous burns. I lit my candle on top of the used wax like always, which ignited two or three other wicks that had remained from the previous burns. It looked like a teepee of flame on the lid. I don't feel worried about it, but if anyone has insight, it would be nice to hear.

— Cherry4

Sometimes the bottom of a new candle will merge with the wax of previous candles and ignite. If there are too many wicks gathered on the jar, I remove them, but sometimes I leave a few together. Then a swell in flame will occur, with the wax feeding all the wicks at once. I take this as a naturally occurring process if one has chosen to burn candles on a sugar or honey jar without a candle stand and without cleaning off the old wicks. I view it in a generally positive light. It is a sight to behold though, and I am glad you witnessed it, because it could be dangerous if unattended.

— Joseph Magnuson (M)

• The lid on my honey jar came off. Is it ruined?

I went to put my honey jar away and as i was trying to pick up the jar my finger must've touched the lid and it flew open. Does that mean that energy is now lost?

— MaJiG_GarDen

I am of the Try It & See Tribe. If it continues to work as well as before, you'll know. If it was affected by the mishap, you can make a new one.

— CopperFox

• What do I do with a leaky honey jar?

I packed my honey jar in my suitcase and I didn't tighten it completely so honey leaked out during the flight. Do I have to redo it?

— y2241

If you felt inclined you could simply re-open it, and add some honey.

— starsinthesky7 (M)

• **How much is too much?**

I had been talking to a guy every day for a couple of weeks and thought things were great and then it suddenly stopped. He would not say a word to me or explain why. I figured a honey jar spell wouldn't hurt. So far there has been no response. The strongest candle sign came when I dressed and burned a red candle on the night of a full moon and lunar eclipse. I added Queen Elizabeth root shavings to my incense plates and a small glass heart to each plate as well. Still no response.

I added Crown of Success and Chuparrosa vigil candles around the honey jar. Rather than asking for things to be brought into my life, I asked for the negative to be removed via a petition-paper dressed with herbs.

I also burned a combo of Come to Me Incense, Queen Elizabeth root shavings, and Love Herbs Mix. I tried contacting my intended and got no response. I added a John the Conqueror root to my mojo bag and the honey jar. I put a lodestone nearby.

My latest candle tonight ended with bright tall flame for several minutes and then spontaneously died down and out. Still no response.

— joyfulgrl

I think you are doing quite a bit for someone you don't really have a relationship with, but just liked and talked to for a few weeks.

Maybe you are obsessing too much over him. I think now you have to let it go and trust that Spirit will take care of your petition. If after a certain period of time, and in your case I would not give it more than a few weeks, if no progress is made (and I don't mean mere signs in flames and wax), you should move on, and concentrate on attracting the right person, someone you may not even know, into your life.

If you switch gears to 'attracting the right person' I would not even Cut and Clear, unless you have such strong emotional ties to this first person that it is holding you back. Who knows? Maybe at some point the first person may come back into your life, but right now is not the time for it.

— Keirith

God's plan is invariably better than ours, so why such a tight focus? Your spells are strong and indicate that you want and intend to find true love. Follow Keirith's advice, broaden the work, and let the right one in!

— deaconmillett (M, AIRR)

• How popular and how successful are honey jars?

I'm really interested in buying a honey jar to use to have a friend sweeten to me. Before I consider purchasing one, I would like to know if any one has used them in the past or is currently using one now and have they been very successful or unsuccessful?

— Daytona12

Honey jar spells have been used for hundreds of years and are being used now by thousands of people. How successful yours will be for you will depend upon many factors: How strong you are, how much faith you have in it working, how good a choice a sweetening spell is for the friend you have in mind, and how dedicated you are at working it. If you're not confident, you may be better off having a light set for you. If you feel confident that you can do this, then *go honey jar*!

— NotDorianGray

• Can someone be immune to sweetening?

Can someone resist the sweetening effects of a sugar, syrup, or honey jar? I know these spells are powerful and positive but I'm wondering if people have been able to resist the effects?

— Daytona12

There are lots of rumours of people having immunity or resistance to magic. I've worked with the occult since I was a kid and I'll tell you that no Dungeons and Dragons or comic book style resistance exists. Some people are harder to work on than others. They may have natural defenses, unconscious barriers, or even magical protections in place, but usually they can still be influenced.

There are a myriad other factors involved beyond resistance. The spell-caster may not be experienced or may be approaching the target from the wrong angle. For example, if I am trying to sweeten a relative, and the work manifests slowly because the person is just too mad, I would calm the anger first with Peace Water, then heal any rifts, and finally work on the honey jar. As in war, strategy is required. Look at your target, find the best angle of approach, and go for it. Your magic only fails when you fail.

— ConjureMan Ali (M, AIRR)

• What are these black bits in my candle wax?

I burnt my candle on a honey jar. It was burning cleanly until 3/4 down. When i went back to the room i found a small black object in the candle wax as it was burning. I have no idea what it is. It could be a bug that flew into it, or a piece of the wick. Should I leave it in the candle holder?

— LMgroupie

Many candle wicks will form black bits of ash on them as they burn. Unless the wick does this to an unusual degree (causing the flame to get too high, for example), this is part of a normal burn, although one may certainly look for signs in the shapes that are formed. Also, many insects are attracted to light and thus fly too close to a flame and die. For the sake of fire safety, it is a good idea to clean your candle holders regularly between burns.

— Lukianos (M, AIRR)

• How would I use a honey jar to attract a new lover?

I was just looking in "Hoodoo Herb and Root Magic" at the entry on honey jars. The entry says that a honey jar spell can be used to attract a new lover. I only ever heard of sweetening spells working on specific people you already know. How would one go about making a honey jar to attract a new lover?

— Jason82 (AIRR)

The major differences in attracting and sweetening a new or unknown person versus attracting and sweetening a known person are the content of the name-paper and the absence of personal concerns.

To make a petition to draw a sweet new love, you would construct the petition as usual, but in the place of the known lover's name, you would write instead "my unknown lover / perfect partner / wife / husband / friend-with-benefits," or whatever kind of person you wished to manifest. You may open the jar and add names (or remove them) as you wish.

Candles may also be varied in support of your work. You may burn white candles for an unknown love, and after you meet a likely person, you may burn pink candles for friendship, then red candles for intimacy.

— Lukianos (M, AIRR)

• Is it okay that my daughter spilled wax on top of my jar?

I need some advice. I started a honey jar spell today and my candle has been burning VERY clean with hardly any drips, just a very clean burn. Is this a good sign? Also later this evening, my daughter walked in to my room and picked up the jar slightly and put it back down which may have caused a very slight wax spill onto the jar top. Does this interfere with the honey jar, or is it okay to continue? Do I place the new candle back on top of the candle residue from today's candle?

—heaven

If it burns clear, that's a good sign. Some wax can spill on the lid. It is okay that your daughter touched it. Yes, you place the candle back on top of the candle residue. Some people's honey jar spells have layers of wax on them because they like working with that honey jar so much.

— starsinthesky7 (M)

• What does it mean when the wick bends?

I burned a candle for my honey jar. and the wick seemed to bend. As the wick was bending it then curled and formed a heart shape. Does this have any significance?

— MaJiG_GarDen

Wicks naturally bend when they burn, so that's normal. A heart shape might be a good indication, so I say keep the thoughts positive.

— Tabbylove17

• What should I do if the honey does not move?

I have a honey jar for my ex-boyfriend's friends and one for his family, but the honey in their jars does not move. I found this strange because I did one for my ex the same week and his honey is still active.

— spellyshelly

Your ex is easier to sweeten than his friends and family. I don't view movement within the jar as movement in the work.

— deaconmillett (M, AIRR)

• **What if the name-paper becomes torn?**

I did a sweetening spell, and after a few weeks of candle burning, I just saw that the name-paper inside the jar somehow got torn! Nope, I didn't open the jar or shake it. Jar's made of glass, and I can see through the maple syrup that the name-paper has got a split on it. Is it a sign?

— Jinglepop

If you did it yourself subconsciously or if it happened by other means, I would think that someone does *not* want your work to happen. Either your target was being protected from what you were aiming to do, or someone took direct action and worked against you. I would take out the paper and redo it, adding lemon grass and Road Opener or Van Van Oil.

— Dr Johannes (M, AIRR)

• **What can a city girl do with her honey jar?**

I want to bury my honey jar to be walked over, but there is concrete outside both doors to my building, and no way to put a honey jar under my floor boards, either. Any suggestions for a city girl?

— Jeannie M.

Bury it in a potted plant, whether a house plant or one on the balcony, and nurture the plant to keep it alive and thriving.

— pma

I tend to get a little worried when a plant I use in a spell eventually dies, so I'd suggest that you buy a small sack of cement, and a terracotta pot or a bucket. The pot can be plain or fancy, as you choose. You can add cowrie shells to your shopping list if you wish.

The honey jar goes into the pot first. Mix the cement and fill the pot completely, covering up the jar inside. Maybe add some cowrie shells to the top and outside for good looks. Let it dry, paint it if it is not already well-glazed, and you've made your hidden honey jar into a nice little sculptural addition to the bedroom or the altar. You can use it as a statuary stand or a stand for decorative pillar candles.

That's the urban version. It will blend nicely with that environment.

— Dr Johannes (M, AIRR)

• **The wax on my jar is uneven. What does it mean?**

I have noticed that there has been wax residue on my honey jar but the left side has way more residue than the right. What does it mean?
— Lulu

Is the top an even surface or does it have dents in it? If the flame is being moved by a draft, that can affect things as well. Is it a sign? I would say no. Candle burning is exciting when you are doing it for the first time, but not everything is a sign. Sometimes it is…what it is.
— starsinthesky7 (M)

• **What does wax runoff mean?**

Sometimes the candle wax runs down the jar, other times it burns clean. He's away again with the other woman. Does running wax mean he cries for me or that she's crying? This time it hasn't been me doing the crying.
— hoodoo curious

Candle divination is subjective so I usually advise to not look for anything, but if something jumps out at you, then take note of it. Some candles burn clean and some leave much residue. How much wax runs down is contingent upon the type of candle you are using, but as you noted, it usually means that there are tears involved. As to whose tears; well, that may be the subject of a divination. Consider getting a reading.
— ConjureMan Ali (M, AIRR)

• **What does a pool of wax mean?**

Is it possible to have just a fluke when burning the candles on the jar? So far there had been nothing left at all and then today's candle left a good pool of wax on the lid and a stream of wax down one side of jar.
— hoodooTom

I caution against reading too much into candle burns unless you are familiar with ceromancy. Look for generalities and stay confident no matter what happens. The wax may be a sign that becomes apparent later.
— ConjureMan Ali (M, AIRR)

• **What does it mean if I burn my finger?**

About two weeks ago I opened a honey jar that had two pictures in it of my lover and I. While I was burning the pictures I accidentally burned my finger with his picture. Someone told me it means bad luck.

— bella6

Well, since the only reason for burning the pictures that had been lovingly nestled in a jar of honey would be to actively destroy the spell of sweetness, then getting burned by the flame from one of the pictures would indicate that you had succeeded in destroying all of the person's sweetness for you and replacing it with angry flaming rage.

Consider getting a half-hour coaching session with a member of AIRR. You may benefit from the guidance of an experienced worker.

— nagasiva (M)

• **What does it mean if a pink candle burns faster than a red one?**

I lit a pink candle and a red candle on the honey jar simultaneously. The pink one burned much faster than the red one. Same size, and I lit them at the same time, but the pink burned completely down and the red looked as if I had just lit it. What could this mean?

— Angel09

Pink for friendship and romance, red for lust and passion. Pink burns fast, red burns very slow. Romance and friendship will develop more quickly than lust and passion.

— catherineyronwode (M, AIRR)

• **Is it okay to do more than one honey jar at a time?**

I'm trying to work a spell to reconcile with an ex and to bring my parents closer together. I heard that more than one honey jar is a mistake.

— SylvrDyamond

If the situations differ, use two jars. I have quite a few successful honey jars going right now for various situations and they work wonderfully.

— Literarylioness (M)

• **Can I use a honey jar to win the lottery or get money?**

Can anyone tell me if I can use the lottery logo in my state to do a honey jar sweetening spell to possibly win money in the lotto or lottery?

— mysiclady

I see why you might think that a honey jar is appropriate, but I don't think that in this case it would get you the results that you want and here's why: A honey jar is used to sweeten an individual or an organization to you. So you might well succeed in making the state lotto organization love you, but unless you think that they are really loading the game and hand selecting the winners, I wouldn't bother. Usually whether they like you or not has no bearing on whether or not you win the money.

— Miss Bri (M, AIRR)

I use a honey jar for drawing money — from clients. I put a sprinkle of Money Drawing Incense on the top of a green tea light (dressed with Money Drawing, Steady Work, and Money Stay With Me Oil) and I set the tea light on top of my honey jar. It has worked for me. I love the smell and I have watched each tea light *spark* just like a sparkler.

— Miss Tammie Lee (M)

• **How specific should my target be?**

Would it be better to sweeten a specific target or to do something more like a love-attracting spell?

— silverfingers

The first spell I did (I was 4.5 years old, but it was a very powerful spell actually) was *very* focused. I wanted a little sister and I was very *detailed.* And I got exactly what I wanted down to hair and eye colour. My mom should not have been able to get pregnant but she did and voila! I even picked the birthdate I wanted her to be born on, disregarding the fact that it would make her six weeks premature. Sure enough, she was born on the day I chose. So when a new spell-caster is trying to decide the best approach, I say, go with specific. The more specific you are, the better the focus and the more tangible the result.

— Miss Bri (M, AIRR)

• What personal concerns are good for sweetening the boss?

I need a raise on the job. I have a photo of my boss and me. For this honey jar spell, what can I add to this photo to make the spell stronger, since I have no other personal items of my boss?

— redacepilot

If you can get his signature, you may have several options:

1) Use the signature paper to write your petition, by crossing and covering the signature with your petition.

2) Fold the signature paper and photo around selected herbs, roots, minerals, or other curios that are appropriate to the situation, creating a packet to place into the jar of sugar or honey.

3) Dip the signature in honey and embed it near the bottom of a sugar jar. Use this sugar to cook foods for the target, leaving the honey-soaked signature near the bottom and replacing sugar in the jar as you go.

— catherineyronwode (M, AIRR)

• Confused about Red Apple Spells?

I'm confused about apple spells. In Cat's book, I read that an apple filled with honey can be buried in a couple's yard. Then there is an apple underneath a potted plant watered with Holy Water and given as a gift. But online she says a candle is lit on a sugar-filled apple, or that the apple is filled with sugar in a container and the candle is lit on the container.

— thegoldman

I read about burning a pink candle on the top of a cored apple, with a name-paper inside the apple. You burn the candle for seven days, then bury the apple. There are different variations of this spell, I think.

— cabriellenil

Sugar and honey spells featuring red Apples and red Onions come in many variations, with or without containers and burial, with or without candles, and with or without potted plants. There is no ONE way to perform these spells any more than there is ONE way to bake a cake. Choose your favourite, because all of them are wonderful!

— catherineyronwode (M, AIRR)

• Can I use my honey jar to attract both friends and a soulmate?

I ordered a honey jar to attract my soulmate. Can I use it at the same time to attract good friends into my life? If so, what do I need to add?

— candis

Use a separate honey jar altogether. The intent is completely different.

— Devi Spring (M, AIRR)

• What to put in a honey jar for a job interview?

I am doing a honey jar spell for a job I am really interested in. All i have is the HR person's business card, and another plain card where she wrote her name and email for me. Which card should i use?

Also the web page on honey jars say we have to eat some of it as we make room for the paper. What if there is already room in the jar?

— zee

For the honey jar, use the paper with her writing. Overwrite it with your name in the traditional way. Even if there is room in the jar, yes, take a spoonful of the honey. While you eat it, focus on how sweet success is and how sweet and attractive (job-wise) you appear to her.

I would advise a simple cleansing bath before the interview itself. Very lightly dress yourself with Crown of Success Oil at the crown of your hair (just a dab!) and Attraction Oil on the very tips of your fingers (to make contact when you shake hands). Just keep fragrances to a minimum, because you don't want to offend anyone's sense of smell.

— CopperFox

• Can you make a honey jar without your own name?

Can I do a honey jar but not put my name over theirs on the petition?

—Blueberry

Yes, you can make a honey jar without putting your name in the jar. You can just put the person's name-paper or picture in the jar. You are sweetening *them*, not yourself.

— MaryBee (M)

• Can a honey jar be used to stop gossip?

My husband wants to put the names of his co-workers into a honey jar. We've been using Stop Gossip Oil but need to make the job less stressful.
— Paradox

Write each name on a separate piece of paper. Place chia seeds and slippery elm bark in each packet. Pray over each one and put them in the honey jar. Dress the candles with Stop Gossip and Tranquility Oil.
— deaconmillett (M, AIRR)

• Is my ex-girlfriend's honey jar messing with me?

I'm not a big proponent of rituals and whatnot, but recently my ex-girlfriend decided that we should do a "forgive-and-forget" honey jar to help reconcile our differences. We shared some of the honey and I've been anointing a pink candle with Road Opener Oil and burning it on top of the sealed honey jar. I normally wouldn't question her on something like this, but lately she has not been very honest with me. She had a sexual relationship with one of my roommates and says that doing a ritual to get him to be more attracted to her was a big part of it. That has ended (or at least I think it has) and she says she wants to work on us again.
— Mujo256

Just some clarification: She had a sexual relationship with your roommate? Do you think you could get past that? Can you be with her even if she's slept with your roommate? These are questions to ask yourself. You should also probably find out what herbs she included in the honey jar. It's important to examine a person's actions so as to ascertain their real intentions. A person could say they want to get back together with you, but if they are also trying to get other people attracted to them, then obviously their actions are not in accord with their claims.

Get a reading. There may be nothing to worry about, but remember that conjure work involves a great deal of sneaky tricks. If she is not honest about her work, it isn't always a bad thing, considering by nature we occults are very secretive. In the context of a relationship where both people are involved in the occult, however, this could be an issue.
— ConjureMan Ali (M, AIRR)

• **When should I quit working my sugar bowl?**

I did the version of the sugar bowl that is in Miss Cat's book for my ex whom i had not spoken to due to an argument and me becoming fed up. I burned the candle for nine days and on the twelfth day he suddenly appeared again on my friends list and sent me a message asking if I was still upset with him.

I said no (I still am a bit, though) and he replied that he was glad to hear that. He then proceeded to ask me about my family and myself. It was short really and I didn't want to sound desperate. Two days later I started a conversation and again kept it short. I feel my trust should be won again at least or some effort made on his part.

But now it's been a week and no more talk, no more messages, and I don't know if I am supposed to keep lighting the candles in the sugar bowl or make a mojo to carry, or what to do.

I guess I'm confused because the sugar bowl was to return him to me and in a way he has, I guess, since now he is on my messenger list and we spoke. So does that mean the spell is done?

— Brujita Angelical

An important part of reconciliation conjure is learning to forgive and being forgiven; it is for this reason we include herbs like balm of Gilead.

I've noticed a commonality amongst reconciliation work that failed, lasted only a brief time, or worked only part-way, and that is that the client would put conditions on the work. "They have to come to me." "They have to make more of an effort." This type of mind-set sabotages the work.

I also don't know how many times I have walked someone through a reconciliation and realized that while they wanted their ex back, they spent the entire time working their spells while they were angry. In your case, you as much as tell us, "I said I wasn't upset, but I still am."

Instead of anger, try to feel the love and longing that drew you to him in the first place, and use that as motivation for your work.

You have received some pretty decent results. Think about it: You went from no contact to contact being established … by him. Now, it's time to let go of some of your hurt and anger. Don't set tough conditions, and don't stay upset. Trust your work and reach out to him.

— ConjureMan Ali (M, AIRR)

• Can I use a quill pen? Can I do a honey jar on five at once?

I want to be friends with five other girls. Is it possible for me to get them all in one honey jar? I plan to use Dove's Blood Ink to write my petition, but I can't write the petition circle without lifting up the quill pen.
— y2241

Print a large photo of yourself that the five photos can be stuck to. When using a quill pen, just write up a petition-paper that does not require a continuous line of text. One honey jar will suffice for all five.
— Devi Spring (M, AIRR)

• Can I let my boyfriend touch my honey jar? Will it ever spoil?

Is it okay to keep a honey jar for good — won't the honey spoil? Should I place the candle in a holder, or just stick it upright to the jar with some melted wax? What can I do to ensure that the wax doesn't run onto my table? My boyfriend knows that I'm doing spells that have to do with him (and he's happy to let me do so). Is it okay for him to touch the jar?
— silver_disc

I've had a honey jar on me and my fiance for almost six years now. Some of the honey has crystallized, but it's fine. I stick candles straight onto the jar. You can put foil underneath your jar or buy a nice saucer to set the jar on that will be its "home." It will catch stray wax. Why wouldn't it be okay for him to touch the jar? It's for both of you, and if you both are participating in the spell, so much the better.
— Devi Spring (M, AIRR)

• Can I add personal concerns to an apple spell?

Can I add personal concerns from both parties and some love herbs along with the honey that is put in a cored-apple spell for reconciliation?
— thegoldman

Yes, you can add personal concerns to an Apple — that personalizes and links the spell to you and the one with whom you seek to reconcile.
— catherineyronwode (M, AIRR)

• Matching skin colour?

Can I use molasses instead of honey, and can I mix it? My boyfriend is black and I thought to match his skin, so if I was to mix it, I would also add maple syrup, brown sugar, and cinnamon. Will this work?

— splitpea

When i was young, it was completely normal to match the skin colour — nowadays people don't all do it, but it actually can add a nice personalizing touch.

I remember one older Black woman telling me how she had once made a healing jar on the sickly little baby of the White woman she cleaned house for. She said she had used white powdered sugar in a baby food jar to represent the healing of the baby, because he had very fair skin. (The powdered sugar was white, like the child; it resembled baby powder; and she kept it in a baby food jar.) In addition to this work, she regularly wiped the baby down with a blessed prayer cloth from her church. He lived, too — and she credited herself with keeping him alive through her prayers until he finally began to grow and put on weight like a normal baby. She had never told his mother that she did these things, for fear of being fired. Guessing from her age when she told me the story, around 1966 or so, this probably had happened in the 1930s, down South, before she moved to the Bay Area.

Just an old memory ...

— catherineyronwode (M, AIRR)

• What do you do with a honey jar if you change your mind?

What should be done with a honey jar when you change your mind about your original intent? For example, if you make a honey jar to reconcile a long standing friendship that soured when you became lovers, and then decide that you actually don't want to reconcile at all, ever?

—GoddessMojo

Rootworker Professor Porterfield taught me to empty the contents of the honey jar at a crossroads and pay the Spirit of the Crossroads nine dimes in thanks for taking the energy of the honey jar for me.

— MaryBee (M)

• What to do with my honey jar on vacation?

After doing the nation sack and the honey jar spell, I have to say that things are beginning to improve quite a bit. I told my husband a little about the honey jar spell, and he approved of it, adding sincerely his hope for it to work. I'm going out of town for a couple of weeks to visit family, and he's unable to come with me due to work reasons. Can I "charge up" the work in advance and leave it?

— Purrness

Why don't you take the nation sack with you? It is common to wear it on your person anyway. Since your husband is in favour of your honey jar, I would just instruct him on how to do it if you are worried about it being worked while you are away. It probably wouldn't hurt if you didn't — I have not always worked mine daily.

— MysticRootworker

• Can I work a honey jar on myself?

I had a painful breakup months ago which has really put a dent in my self-esteem. I was actually thinking of doing a honey jar on myself to love myself more. Has anyone used the honey jar for this purpose?

— sweetpea29

Yes, yes, yes, yes, and yes! I have always had a separate honey jar set up for myself. Forever now. My petition was written along the lines of "I'm beautiful, I'm worthy," sort of like a love letter to myself. And I burn it as often as needed, sometimes more than three days a week.

If I'm anxious about stuff I use Tranquility Oil and Powder; if I need a sexy boost I use Look Me Over Oil; if I'm confused, Clarity Oil; if I feel weak, Master Oil. Whatever I feel I'm in need of, I give myself, like taking vitamins. It's the best thing I've ever done.

— suzyparker

While an old-time hoodoo might scoff at this, a similar job has done wonders for me. A Master Key honey jar is my go-to formula for unlocking strength, courage, self-confidence, and perseverance.

— deaconmillett (M, AIRR)

• **Which jar should I eat the honey out of?**

I recently made a honey jar, following the directions of eating a few spoonfuls of honey. I don't use the actual jar the honey comes in — I have jars that I specifically use as honey jars. The herbs and curios that I put into the existing honey jar aren't fully submerged, and some of it got stuck around the sides of the jar. Next time, should I first eat honey from the jar that it came in, and then pour it into the spell jar with the herbs?

— silver_disc

Take a few minutes to think about a spell and think through why each action is being taken. Think of it like a dance — each move has a meaning. Just doing a twirl means nothing by itself; it only takes on beauty and meaning when connected into the flow of other moves, creating an organic whole. Your ritual needs to tell a story, using the energies of the herbs/curios, your actions, and your prayers.

When you do the work, you want to keep everything flowing together so that the ritual actions and your intent build into a powerful whole. Just eating some honey isn't the point. You're inserting your petition-packet with herbs into the honey. (If some herbs fall out and stick to the jar, so what? You're putting those herbs into the jar anyway.) This inserts your situation and wraps it up in the energy of the honey, and as you do it, you get honey on your finger. So you lick the honey from your finger, and you say "as this honey is sweet to me, so will I grow sweet to [name]" or "so will [Name] be sweet to me." You're essentially defining the role of the honey in *that* jar, assigning its purpose and tapping into its energy. You then dress a candle and light it on the jar to put heat onto the energy within the jar and get it moving upwards and outwards into the world to manifest.

So now a series of simple movements has become meaningful within the flow of those actions. The magic is in the making, not in each one of the steps alone. All that being said, if you did things in a completely different order, but had a very clear picture in your mind of the flow of events and the story you were telling by what you were doing, and were completely confident — you would still have a good spell that would work. But it takes clearly understanding the mechanics of what you're doing, the meaning behind each action, and impregnating each act strongly with your intent.

— Devi Spring (M, AIRR)

• How and when do I stop my honey jar?

I've been doing my honey jar and i think it works well. I'm just curious on how and when do i stop it. If, for example, we are okay now, should i just stop lighting candles and not worry that his feeling will ever fade again? Or do i maintain the honey jar forever? And if so, must i burn candles on it three times a week forever?

— ms_krstin

A honey jar is often meant as a permanent, long-term piece of spell work. If your honey jar is working well in producing the desired effects then you just want to keep working it.

Sometimes when I am working on a situation, I will start the jar and burn candles on it every day. Once I see the results that I want or the situation stabilizes, I will go down to burning candles three times a week or once a week as appropriate.

People keep honey jars going for years, but some only light them once a month, or once a year. Putting them away does not "kill" them.

— Miss B

From one experience I had with a honey jar for a lover…

I worked the jar — and while there remained an attraction, things just didn't work out,which was very much for the best. I put the jar away when I was cleaning one day, and completely forgot about it.

Even though this guy and I had both agreed that seeing each other was no longer appropriate or desirable, every few weeks he would call me out of the blue, saying that he simply couldn't get me out of his mind, had to see me, etc.

I couldn't understand why he was so hung up on me in such a weird way — guys don't ever really have that reaction to me. Then I was looking for something one day and found the months-old honey jar I had made for him. I couldn't believe that I had forgotten to release it and dispose of it! Oops! I did so right away.

I ran into the guy a few days later and he apologized for being so weird the past few weeks and said that he wouldn't bother me like that again. And he never did!

If you no longer want your honey jar working — undo it!

— Devi Spring (M, AIRR)

• **How do I turn a work honey jar into a love honey jar?**

I've been working a Lucky Mojo Boss Fix honey jar for couple of months with great success. Now I want to turn our working relationship into a romantic relationship. I have bunch of love oils and herbs. Can I add them to my Boss Fix honey jar and burn pink or red candles?

— 2010luckyme

In my opinion, you should make a different honey jar since your intention has changed. Try using the Lucky Mojo Love Me honey jar.

— jwmcclin (M)

• **How do I dispose of my honey jar so we are not willed by it?**

I now want to dispose of a honey jar because I decided that I want to have our relationship continue without it being willed a certain way.

1. What is the safest way to dispose of the honey jar that won't hurt either of us or our relationship?

2. Will disposing of the jar ruin our relationship or harm our connection if we were going well before the jar?

3. What were other honey jar users' results once they disposed of the jar? Or do most people keep the jar indefinitely?

—meianoite

Actually, honey jars do not "will" anything. You cannot make a person love you with a honey jar. It is either there or it is not. I have a honey jar to keep my interactions with my boyfriend "sweet," which means we do not fight dirty and we keep our relationship in view.

Tons of people make sugar bowls and honey jars for their relationships. Doing so just helps things along. Everyone can use a bit of sweetness. When they dispose of the jars, the spell is stopped. That's all.

If you want to dispose of your honey jar, you have many options. You can open the jar and bury it so that plants and animals have access to it and spread its magic far and wide. You can leave it entombed and bury it. You can open the jar and wash out the contents in a running stream of water. You can pour out the contents into a hole in your yard and take the jar to be recycled. Doing so will not harm you.

— Literarylioness (M)

• How do I destroy a honey jar without a negative impact?

A couple of months back I made a honey jar spell — but I did the jar without our hair or anything. I just crossed our names on paper as directed. Things are going really great between us, and they were even before the honey jar, so I haven't continued to work with the honey jar since I've created it.

As it's a few months later, I'm wondering if we're continuing to go great because it was meant to be or because of the honey jar's influence.

I really want to destroy the honey jar spell at this point — but I don't want us to break up because I might dispose of it improperly. I just want fate alone to guide our relationship's future.

Is there a way to completely destroy the honey jar itself (the jar, the honey, and the name-papers) without it negatively impacting our relationship because I've destroyed it?

If we break up because it's fate's will, it's okay. I just don't want to influence it any by disposing of the jar in an incorrect manner.

— caramella

Destroying the honey jar as if it were something evil isn't exactly called for, and i can see how the idea of doing so might worry you. Rather, i suggest that you can disperse it (open the container for Ants to have), or dispose of it in a respectfully ritual manner, such as emptying the contents into a stream or river and recycling the glass.

— catherineyronwode (M, AIRR)

Pour out the contents in your backyard. Cleanse the jar with Chinese Wash or Florida Water and reuse or recycle it.

— Mama Micki (M)

• What should I do with wax remains?

What should I do with candle drippings that break off the jar?

—mmcpower

For reconciliation, bury them in the front yard. For keeping someone home, the back yard. For job sweetening, at the job site.

— ConjureMan Ali (M, AIRR)

• So after you're done, where do you dispose of your work?

So as long as you keep working the candle, the honey jar will continue to work. After you're done with it, where do you dispose of it? (If I have to keep it, I'm gonna end up with thousands in my house!)

— jwmcclin (M)

As long as you keep burning candles, the honey jar will keep working for you. When the work is complete, you deploy, disperse, or dispose of it similarly to any other bottle spell. Honey jars are good work, so you would probably keep it on your property, buried in an appropriate place. If there is any attraction aspect, use the front door or porch. A completed Boss Fix honey jar could be placed under a potted plant at work.

— J Simulcik

Deployment is a way of setting a spell into permanent ongoingness. Dispersal sends it out into the world. Disposal is a way of closing the spell and ritually eliminating the materials used in its construction.

If a sugar or honey jar is to be ongoing, you have several options for deployment. Leaving the jar sealed and burying it is quite common.

To disperse its influence, take the lid off the jar and encourage Ants to carry its magical message all around the world, or empty the contents into a hole in the ground at a crossroads and recycle the glass jar.

If the spell is to be concluded, you have several options for disposal. Burning in a fire — the most common form of spell disposal — is not suitable to glass jars or chinaware bowls, so the most common way to dispose of a sugar or honey spell is to wash the contents out in a river, the ocean, or other running water, and bring the container home.

The glass may be recycled, but if the container is of value to you — say, for instance, your regular chinaware dinner service sugar bowl or an intact Mason jar used for canning, you would simply put it back into service without any problem.

These and other ways to deploy, disperse, and dispose of conjure work are described in detail at:

LuckyMojo.com/layingtricks.html

Good luck!

— catherineyronwode (M, AIRR)